LIGHTS

CAMERA

SELL

**SALES
TECHNIQUES
FOR
INDEPENDENT
FILMMAKERS**

WRITTEN BY
ALEC TRACHTENBERG

Published by Coast ART Productions LLC
www.coastartproductions.com

Edited by Michael McConnell
Cover Design by U.T. Denzines
Book Interior Design by Pen2publishing

Ordering Information:
Quantity sales: Special discounts are available on quantity purchases by corporations, associations, and others. For details directly contact the publisher.

Orders by US trade bookstores and wholesalers: Please contact the publisher.

Library of Congress Control Number: 2020916883

ISBN Paperback: 978-1-7355061-0-4
ISBN Hardback: 978-1-7355061-2-8
ISBN eBook: 978-1-7355061-1-1

Printed in the United States of America

First Edition

PRAISE FOR *LIGHTS, CAMERA, SELL*

"It's called Show Business, not Show Art... Alec superbly teaches the Business."

– Dov S-S Simens, legendary film instructor and
author of *From Reel to Deal: Everything You Need to
Create a Successful Independent Film*

"Alec has effectively conveyed the importance of adopting a sales mindset throughout the filmmaking process. This book is for all of the independent filmmakers out there who are trying to make a name for themselves."

– Matthew Helderman, producer and
CEO of Buffalo 8 & Bondit Media Capital

"*Lights, Camera, Sell* is a roadmap on how artistic and creative types can use sales concepts to elevate their careers."

– Franco Sama, producer and CEO of Samaco Films

"Alec successfully shows us how the outbound sales development strategies found in Silicon Valley technology companies can be directly applied to the daily activities of independent filmmakers across the globe. If you want to accomplish anything in filmmaking you need to embrace sales as a vital skill to learn."

– Aaron Ross, best-selling author of *Predictable
Revenue* and *From Impossible to Inevitable*

"*Lights, Camera, Sell* explores essential sales techniques used by both Fortune 500 and Silicon Valley startups and interprets them in a way that connects with the filmmaking community."

– Jeb Blount, CEO of Sales Gravy and
author of *Fanatical Prospecting*

"This book is a MUST READ... not just for independent filmmakers... it's for everyone. Being creative is just not enough anymore. We need to master the art of selling. Whether you're selling your service, your idea or your film to investors and distributors, you need strategic sales techniques. In this book, that's exactly what you'll get!"

– Suzanne Lyons, producer and author of *Indie Film Producing: The Craft of Low Budget Filmmaking*

"*Lights, Camera, Sell* is a must read for all independent filmmakers who want to make money doing what they love."

– Alex Ferrari, filmmaker & founder of *Indie Film Hustle* and author of *Rise of the Filmtrepreneur: Turn Your Independent Film into a Moneymaking Machine*

"*Lights, Camera, Sell* takes the sting out of sales and shows how it can be a natural part of an artist's life. A must read if you want to get ahead in your career"

– Daniel Pink, New York Times Bestselling author of
To Sell is Human, Drive, and A Whole New Mind

CONTENTS

INTRODUCTION   1

CHAPTER 1: Prospecting   15

CHAPTER 2: Prospecting— A Case Study   33

CHAPTER 3: Discovery   55

CHAPTER 4: Discovery — A Case Study   75

CHAPTER 5: Demonstrate Value   93

CHAPTER 6: Demonstrate Value — A Case Study   109

CHAPTER 7: Closing the Deal   125

CHAPTER 8: Closing the Deal — A Case Study   141

CHAPTER 9: Relationship Success   157

CHAPTER 10: Relationship Success — A Case Study   175

THE FINAL WORD   189

SPECIAL THANKS   195

ABOUT THE AUTHOR   197

INTRODUCTION

L et's be honest. You didn't wake up one day and decide to pursue a career in filmmaking so that you could call yourself a salesperson. Filmmaking is a form of art, and artists are not typically known to be businesspeople, especially not salespeople. Imagine Pablo Picasso trying to peddle his artwork on a street corner, or Martin Scorsese planning a sales presentation and addressing a list of objections from a buyer.

———

A common belief in the filmmaking arena is that agents, managers, and studio executives are the personnel who handle anything business or sales related. Which begs the question: Why would an independent filmmaker even be thinking about learning sales techniques? I'm sure, as you are reading these words, you are thinking, "Sales is the last skillset on Earth I would need to become a successful film producer or director!"

Everyone has had their own experiences with a salesperson at some point in their life, someone who undoubtedly heavily impacted their perception of everything related to sales. All it takes is for one person to sell you something that failed to work to convince you to distrust all future interactions with salespeople. At the end of the day, it is never a great feeling when you realize you have been deceived or lied to in some way.

1

With the amount of disdain toward sales and salespeople, it makes sense why there are only 3 to 5 percent of the 4,000 American colleges offering sales curricula. However, funny enough, around 50 percent of business and marketing majors find themselves in a sales related-occupation. Why, then, is there such a negative bias surrounding sales and the people partaking in this type of venture?

Sketchy character tropes found in films and television shows, and so many recent stories of scams and shady practices, convince many individuals to think of salespeople in a negative way. Whether it's the pushy used-car dealer who will use every possible tactic to sell someone a clunker, or the annoying telemarketer who will consistently call you back a hundred times after you clearly hung up on them, salespeople are commonly perceived to be smooth-talking, desperate, and aggressive.

Take Danny DeVito's character Harry Wormwood in the 1996 feature film *Matilda* as a solid example. Harry is a used-car salesman who will do anything to pull a fast one on any customer willing to fork over their cash. Even the FBI is investigating him on his shady business practices, but this doesn't stop him from ripping people off left and right.

Look no further than the cast of characters in the classic 1992 feature *Glengarry Glen Ross*. The characters played by Al Pacino, Kevin Spacey, and Alec Baldwin display a relentless attitude toward closing deals and winning a sales contest. Alec Baldwin's famous line in this film is when he goes over the ABCs of sales. It can even be argued that he reinforces what most people think salespeople are always thinking when in a conversation with a potential customer: "Always be closing." It's no wonder why many people quickly decline when they are asked by a salesperson if they need help finding something in a store.

Sales is Everywhere

The truth is: sales is found in every aspect of your life. Your ability or inability to effectively influence those around you, through conviction, persuasion, or negotiation, will determine whether you successfully get what you want or not. This can be as simple as persuading your friend to watch one of your favorite movies instead of one they suggest. Or it can be as practical as convincing a future employer on why you are the perfect candidate for the position. Or it can be as serious as negotiating with a hostile individual who is looking to harm yourself or others. The ability to effectively articulate and influence others on your ideas, beliefs, and actions is what sets you apart from the rest. Being able to control an outcome and get others on your side are powerful acts, benefitting not only your business, but also your personal life.

One point of confusion for most people is understanding that sales isn't only a type of profession. It's also a way of life. A majority of people think that because their job title doesn't have the words "Sales" or "Business Development" in it, they are not considered to be in sales. However, every single day, you are selling yourself, your ideas, and your beliefs in some capacity.

For example, in order to convince your girlfriend you are the perfect mate for her, you need to practice sales techniques, which includes listening to your prospect's needs, displaying the value of your product (yourself), and closing the deal by proposing to her. It's not very difficult to notice that the first few dates sometimes feel like a job interview, or better yet, a sales presentation. Sharing information about your likes and dislikes, interests and goals, is a way that you share your "product knowledge." Providing a potential mate with information, such as the make and model of your flashy car, a visit to your fabulous house in a nice neighborhood, and the details of your high-paying or interesting job, highlights the benefits, features, and advantages that set you apart from your competitors.

Children are oftentimes considered the best salespeople because they don't surrender until they get what they want. You can refuse to give in on their desires all you want, but their natural ability to cry, kick, and scream will frequently result in parents caving in. Think about the toys or even the pets you wanted as a child and how you were able to make a case on why this was the best course of action for you and your parents.

Take this same philosophy and think about it in the sense of career development. You can be the smartest person in the room, with the perfect academic record and resume, but if you cannot successfully communicate with the interviewer and persuasively articulate why you are the perfect person for the opportunity, you will not get very far in life. There is no doubt that sales is a skill set every person should aim to learn to not only get the opportunity to advance in all of their endeavors, but to also create a better life for themself and the people they love.

Sales in the World of Filmmaking

Now that it is evident that sales affects every area of our lives, we can narrow this down even further—to the world of independent filmmaking. The terms "independent filmmaking" and "independent filmmaker" encompass films and filmmakers not funded by the major movie studio system, which includes studios like Paramount, Warner Brothers, Fox, etc. Independent projects are usually self-financed or privately financed by one or more individuals or entities. In general, most filmmakers start their career in the low-budget and ultra-low-budget arena of independent filmmaking.

Let's take a look at a few of the most well-known independent filmmakers and the people around them and how the skill set of sales has directly impacted their individual projects and their whole careers.

Quentin Tarantino

Before audiences were able to enjoy the blockbuster fast action hits *Once Upon a Time in Hollywood, Kill Bill,* and *Inglorious Bastards*, Quentin Tarantino started off as a low-budget independent filmmaker. After being persuaded by independent producer Lawrence Bender in the late 1980s to write his first screenplay, which turned out to be the cult classic *True Romance*, Tarantino quickly found himself with more open doors around him. Lawrence Bender tried to persuade Tarantino to write a screenplay after meeting him at a Hollywood party after learning Tarantino knew so many things about films since he worked at a video store. Lawrence Bender's ability to effectively persuade Tarantino to finally write a screenplay led Tarantino to launch a successful screenwriting career.

In 1991, independent producer Lawrence Bender tapped into his network of prospects and sent one of Tarantino's newest scripts to director Monte Hellman, who ultimately helped secure funding for the film through Richard Gladstein at Live Entertainment. *Reservoir Dogs*, which was Tarantino's directorial debut, was screened at the Sundance Film Festival in January 1992. The film turned out to be a huge success, and it further launched his career—not only as a screenwriter, but also a director.

Tarantino had to sell himself as not only a great screenwriter, but also someone who could successfully direct a feature film. Imagine the conversations he must have had while directing his first feature film with his fellow crew members and actors. There was most likely a great deal of him selling everyone on his credibility for the position and his vision of how the story should be conveyed. Did the acts of conviction and persuasion get Tarantino and Bender where they are today? Is there any doubt they networked with their circle of influence and effectively sold their projects to those around them? Absolutely.

David Lynch

Another great independent filmmaker of our time is David Lynch, who is best known for films like *Eraserhead, Mulholland Drive,* and *Blue Velvet.* While enrolled in the Pennsylvania Academy of Fine Arts in Philadelphia in the late 1960s, Lynch was in the process of making one of his first short films while working full-time and having a wife and kids. While making his short film *Six Men Getting Sick (Six Times),* Lynch had to be creative in how he was going to get this film done with the least amount of money. Using a variety of sales skills, Lynch was able to persuade the Academy to use one of its upper rooms as a working space, all while negotiating on a cheaper price for the 16mm camera, sound equipment, and lighting package. Using the leftover money he had from his first short film, Lynch directed another animated short film shortly after, in 1968, titled *The Alphabet*.

When Lynch was finished with post-production, he used his sales skills by understanding the market and finding opportunities for his project. Having been aware of the newly formed American Film Institute (AFI) and its new film grant opportunities, Lynch proceeded to contact the AFI and sent over a copy of the script *The Alphabet*, along with a script to another live action film, *The Grandmother*. Lynch demonstrated his persuasion skills in his film grant submission, which awarded him over eight thousand dollars in financing and a relationship with a major film organization.

In 1971 when Lynch moved to Los Angeles with his wife and kids, Lynch enrolled in the AFI Conservatory. Lynch has stated that the AFI Conservatory was a chaotic and unorganized place that also allowed him to develop one of his first feature-length scripts, titled *Gardenback*. After eventually being fed up with the Conservatory, Lynch dropped out the second year. The Conservatory's dean, Frank Daniel, quickly persuaded Lynch to reconsider coming back to the school to continue working on his project. Lynch agreed on the stipulation that he could create his own project that wouldn't be interfered with, which ultimately turned out to be his first major hit, *Eraserhead*.

If the dean of AFI Conservatory had not effectively sold Lynch on coming back to the program and if Lynch had not conclusively set out the agreement that allowed him to make the project the way he wanted, there would have been no *Eraserhead* movie and most likely no successful filmmaking career for David Lynch. In almost every social situation, there is someone attempting to sell someone else, and in this case, Lynch being sold by Daniel to come back to the Conservatory changed the course of his life for the better.

Robert Rodriguez

Robert Rodriguez is one of the most notable crafty independent filmmakers, and he is another significant example of someone who has used sales skills in his filmmaking pursuits. Born in San Antonio, Texas, in 1968, Rodriguez was raised in a working-class home by his mother and father, who happened to be a cookware salesperson. In his autobiography, *Rebel Without a Crew*, Rodriguez shares the process of making his first feature film, *El Mariachi*, with nothing but $7,000 and a dream. He explains the many ways he bartered with his network of friends and associates for cameras, sound and lighting equipment, and how he was able to secure shooting locations in Northeastern Mexico. He even subjected himself to medical experimentation on multiple occasions to acquire money for the film.

In the end, Rodriguez ultimately created a whole new style of filmmaking called the Mariachi Style, also known as Guerilla Filmmaking, which entails low-budget strategies like having a limited cast and crews and quickly using real locations without obtaining permits. This type of filmmaking has grown in popularity over the years, especially among low-budget filmmakers who may not have the capital to afford two hundred crew members, fifty location permits, and twelve major movie stars.

Originally, the movie was meant to be for the Latino video market as funding for another larger project Rodriguez was contemplating. After being rejected from a variety of Latino straight-to-video distributors, Rodriguez decided to send his film, which was only a trailer at the time, to bigger distribution companies. This gained the attention of Columbia Pictures, which ultimately purchased the film from Rodriguez and spent hundreds of thousands of dollars in post-production work before it was distributed worldwide.

Rodriguez's tactics of tapping into his network for resources, not taking "No" for an answer when Latino distributors turned down his film, and committing to his vision of sharing his film to the world the correct way are all concrete examples of how he heavily influenced the outcome of his project through the medium of sales. Although Rodriguez's job title doesn't have the words "Sales" or "Business Development" in it, it's hard for one to argue that Rodriguez *isn't* in the business of influencing and getting commitments from others.

Steven Spielberg

In the early stages of his career, legendary filmmaker Steven Spielberg used his sales competency of being persistent to get the attention of Universal Studios' vice president at the time, Sidney Sheinberg, which led to Spielberg being the youngest director to be signed for a long-term deal with a major Hollywood studio. At nineteen years old, Spielberg boarded a tour bus at Universal Studios Hollywood, jumped off, snuck into a bathroom, and then disappeared behind a building. Once the tour bus was gone he spent the rest of the day on the Universal lot, exploring film sets and getting immersed in the world he wanted to be a part of.

He eventually bumped into a man named Chuck Silvers, who happened to work in the television department for Universal. Silvers discovered that Spielberg was an aspiring film director, and he ended up writing him a three-day pass to allow him to visit the studio. Spielberg proceeded to go back on the studio lot for three days, and on the fourth day he dressed up in a suit and brought his father's briefcase. At the security gate he confidently said hello to the guards, who waved back and let him in. For three months, Spielberg would arrive at the studio gate, wave to the guards, and walk right through like he owned the place. Sneaking into soundstages and editing rooms, while also taking the time to schmooze with directors and producers, Spielberg even spent the night in an empty office and changed into fresh clothes the next morning.

In time, Silvers convinced Spielberg that schmoozing was one thing, but Spielberg needed to showcase his talent by directing a quality short film. Spielberg was no stranger to creating short films, as he had a track record of making them since he was twelve years old. After months of directing and post-production, Spielberg finished his twenty-six-minute film, called *Amblin*. Vouching for Spielberg, Silvers reached out to Sheinberg and shared Spielberg's work. After watching the film, Sheinberg asked to meet with Spielberg immediately and ultimately offered him a seven-year director's contract on the spot.

Strategic prospecting skills, winning people over through presentation, establishing rapport and trust—these are the movements

Spielberg consciously performed, which are also found in the activities of the world's top salespeople. There is no question Spielberg did his research on the major players around him, including his mentor Chuck Silvers, and most importantly, one of the major bosses at the studio, Sid Sheinberg. Wearing a suit and bringing his father's suitcase to the studio lot is a demonstration of him using personal image to convey confidence and convince others he belonged there as much as everyone else around him.

But Who am I?

Many of you are rightfully asking, "Who are you to try to connect sales and filmmaking?" I would be asking the same question. My name is Alec Trachtenberg, and I have been *selling* practically all of my life. Born and raised in New York, I have had a street-smart hustler mentality since day one. When I was in fifth grade, my mom had to pick me up at my school's principal's office because I had been illegally downloading music from websites like LimeWire and Kazaa and selling CD-ROMs to my classmates. It definitely wasn't the most ethical way to make money, but that day I knew: a life of entrepreneurship and selling was for me.

When I was thirteen, I came up with more acceptable ways of generating cash. This was a time when Myspace was the craze, and I was charging fifty dollars to anyone who wanted me to remodel their Myspace profiles with beautiful graphics and designs. My Myspace designing skills led me to other business opportunities. I built a relationship with a Las Vegas promoter and was closing bottle service and hotel packages and receiving monthly checks in the mail. My mother couldn't believe that I—at such a young age—was getting paid like this.

Fast-forward to my time in the professional world. I have been an account executive and sales manager at a variety of companies in the technology, entertainment, and digital marketing space for over a decade. Throughout the years, I have sold to such clients as Netflix, Amazon, and Airbnb as well as small neighborhood clients like a mom-and-pop bookstore. Having worked at an array of companies that offer digital marketing and technology solutions, I have been able to establish close connections with my clients and deliver powerful ways to solve their business problems and ways to market themselves to a captive audience. I am an active salesperson who practices what I preach, and I have doubled and tripled the revenue of the companies I have worked for and for my clients. I have managed sales teams and have built effective sales collateral, including email and call scripts, that have led to millions of dollars in closed revenue. In addition, I consult and coach freelancers, small business owners, and entrepreneurs from all walks of life and show them how to multiply their profits.

What does any of this have to do with independent filmmaking? Not only do I live and breathe sales, I also happen to be an independent filmmaker. I have always been captivated by all things Hollywood, and I knew at an early age that I wanted to produce films. Since 2012, I have made a series of short films and a feature film under my production company, Coast ART Productions. I produced my first feature film, *The Cabin* (2018), in a small rural town in Sweden, three hours north of Stockholm. With funding acquired from the Swedish government and from our Kickstarter supporters, my co-producer and director, Johan Bodell, and I set out to make our first feature film no matter what it took. We casted our actors and director of photography in Los Angeles and flew everyone to Sweden, where we shot the film in four weeks. We eventually facilitated a distribution deal, and I am proud to say our film is available to hundreds of millions of people via digital streaming.

During my filmmaking ventures, I eventually realized that there is plenty of overlap in what I have practiced in my day job as a salesperson. I was identifying opportunities, building rapport with cast and crew, demonstrating value through demo reels and pitch decks, striking agreements through contracts, resolving on-set conflicts, and more. Since sales is a skillset that everyone practices on a daily basis, regardless whether they are aware of it or not, I decided to take my experience and knowledge of sales that I have acquired working in the technology, digital marketing, and entertainment space and help other independent filmmakers in utilizing sales techniques for their benefit. Independent filmmaking is an unpredictable journey filled with heartaches and triumphs, and there are a lot of things I wish someone told me before I set out to make my first micro-budget feature film.

The Sales Process in Independent Filmmaking

In this book I will walk you through a five-step sales process and provide specific examples of how you can perform each stage within the framework of independent filmmaking. I will follow up each stage in the sales process with specific examples on how you can perform some of these sales techniques in your conversations with writers, crew members, actors, financiers, and distributors.

Over the years I have read a plethora of how-to books on independent film producing. However, I have found that none of these books personally supplies the necessary sales techniques a filmmaker must use to their benefit. Throughout these pages, I will share a series of sales techniques to use in the independent filmmaking process, which will help you influence and gain commitment from others on yourself, your ideas, and your beliefs.

Whether it's being able to effectively convince a screenwriter you are the exemplary producer to bring their story to life, or being able to negotiate with a producer on the final edit of your masterpiece, the sales techniques you will learn in this book will ultimately help you in your filmmaking endeavors. Additionally, this book is designed for the self-employed filmmakers, from editors to script supervisors, who are trying to land their next gig. At the end of this book, my goal is for you to change the way you perceive sales in general, along with starting to embrace the idea that to be a successful independent filmmaker, you must identify yourself as a salesperson.

Important Note

Before we get started, I want to clarify that I will be using the words "project" and "product" interchangeably throughout this book to represent your film project. Your film project can be a feature film, television show, online series, etc. I will also be using the words "prospect" and "client" interchangeably throughout each of the stages. This can be anyone from a film financier or distributor to an actor, crew member, screenwriter, producer, and more.

Let's get started!

STAGE I

PROSPECTING

CHAPTER 1
PROSPECTING

Defining Prospecting

To better understand what the process of prospecting is, one can look no further than where the term originated from. The term *prospector* refers to an individual who searches for mineral deposits through drilling and excavation. This was famously done during the California Gold Rush in the mid-1800s. When spots of gold were discovered, the prospectors would spend time sifting through the dirt to find the treasured nuggets of gold left behind when the dirt was washed away.

As the first step in the sales process, you are doing the same task of finding pieces of gold in massive amounts of dirt. The gold the salesperson is in search of is a qualified customer who would benefit from the salesperson's product. Modern-day sales prospecting is doing extensive research and sifting through a large list of potential buyers to try to uncover those who are interested and ready to buy.

Prospecting Goals

Prospecting is oftentimes the area most salespeople rush through or overlook. However, it is one of the most important stages to ensure you are:

- Connecting with the ideal person and/or company

- Decreasing the amount of wasted time with people who don't benefit from the value of your project or service

- Using your research to communicate your knowledge of your prospect's background and experience

Types of Prospects

Unless someone has previously done business with you, it's a complete unknown if this person is interested in what you have to bring to the table. Because prospects are not considered customers yet, you can break prospects into two different categories:

- **Suspects:** These are people whom you think may need your products or services but may not be aware of you and your offerings. They can potentially be a future client of yours, but you are not sure. In order to find out, you must reach out to them and increase awareness and familiarity of yourself and your business. Once they are aware, it's time for them to decide if they may do business with you in the future.

- **Prospects:** These are the individuals you have made contact with. Whether it's in-person or through email, these are the people who have expressed potential interest in what you have to offer. Examples of this would include a man in a shoe store who is looking for a new type of running shoe, or a young couple interested in viewing a timeshare so they can have a residence during their vacation.

Prospecting Methods

There are a variety of communication tools you can use during your prospecting endeavors to ensure you are increasing awareness and familiarity of yourself and your business offerings. These include:

- **Phone calls:** Second best to having a conversation in-person, phone calls are a great way to initiate a dialogue while also being able to convey tone and emotion through the use of your voice.

- **Automated Voicemail Messages:** Voicemail is designed to distribute information and lure the prospect to take some sort of action, such as calling you back or going to a specific website.

- **Text:** Texting is a great way to get a short message across. Although texting has grown in popularity over the years, it is looked down upon to send long-form messages to elicit any sort of action from your prospect. Providing the best number to call or best email address to reach you (or confirmation of a specific address to meet you) is acceptable.

- **Email:** One of the most popular ways to professionally reach out to a prospect, an initial email can include specific attachments like documents, pictures, and other media to articulate who you are and what you are offering.

- **Direct Mail:** Not such a popular tool nowadays, mail can still be a creative and different approach, setting you apart from others. Sometimes providing a hard copy of your sales collateral sitting on their desk will result in a prospect paying more attention to it.

Steps to Prospecting

Like the process of sales, prospecting consists of multiple steps. These three key steps include: research, outreach, and scheduling a discovery call.

Step #1: Research

How do you measure the difference between a poor introductory meeting and a successful one? It's simple: have context.

By researching potential prospects before you first call or email them can make the difference between closing a deal and going bust.

By using research methods and taking the time to understand the background of the individual you are about to speak to, you can better frame the conversation and set you apart from the dozens of other conversations the prospect is having on a daily basis. By creating relevancy, you are more likely to get a prospect's attention and have a beneficial conversation.

You wouldn't waste time with a particular feature-film distributor if you found out comedy and family films are not their specialty. You wouldn't take a call with an actress if you discovered she is a nightmare to work with and ultimately will make your life a living hell. Lastly, you wouldn't work with a camera rental shop with a swarm of one-star reviews and numerous reports of sketchy business practices. These are all specific examples you can avoid in the research phase of prospecting.

How to Conduct Research

Putting on your research hat does NOT mean you need to spend countless hours stalking this person's social media accounts and trying to identify the names of his children. While there is plenty of information to gather from your research ventures, there are only a handful of main areas you need to focus on:

- **Personal Resume and Work Experience:** Typing the prospect's name on Google will populate a mountain of results. To keep it simple, you should first focus on websites like LinkedIn, IMDb, and personal resume and portfolio websites. Researching what projects they have worked on, the company they currently work for, and the people they have worked with in the past are all subjects that will aid you in understanding who you are about to speak to. Before reaching out to a director of photography, it would be beneficial to see what projects he has worked on in the past and even watch a copy of his demo reel on his website. Some examples of areas you can research include the number of films this person worked on in the past, the prospect's geographic location, how long this person has been in their particular field, etc.

- **Notable Connections:** On websites like LinkedIn, you have the ability to see the number of connections you share with the prospect. Hollywood is a smaller world than most people think, and identifying this crossover in connections can prove it. On websites like IMDb Pro, you can also see if a prospect shares connections with anyone listed on either of your previous IMDb credited projects. Networking is a powerful instrument, and being able to identify connections will ultimately open more doors for you.

- **Company Background:** When speaking with individuals who work for companies or even own a company, such as a post-production supervisor or a film financier, it would be advantageous to do some initial research on the company the individual either owns or works for. Some areas of research on the company you can focus on include the current number of employees, the types of product and services the company offers, the company's list of clients, the year the company was formed, and more. Companies usually have something called a mission statement on their website. A mission statement is a formal summary articulating the values and goals of the organization. This information can be very useful when it comes time to talk about what your project or company goals are, and how they connect with the company the prospect either works for or owns.

- **Media Attention—On or Off the Internet:** This includes everything from internet, newspaper, television, and podcast interviews. When someone gets interviewed, it's usually centered on them or their ventures, and most of the time it's for a positive reason. Sometimes, however, it can be centered on something bad, which would be beneficial for you to be aware of. Bad publicity can be anything from negative remarks said or physical actions by the prospect and will heavily impact the nature of the prospect at the time. Sources like *Variety, Hollywood Reporter,* and *IndieWire* are a few of the many media outlets your prospect can gain attention from. Arming yourself with this knowledge before reaching out to them is instrumental in eliciting a positive response from your outreach.

Building an Ideal Customer Profile

While doing your research, it's important to also identify what your ideal customer profile looks like. For example, when attempting to find a soulmate, it would make sense for a person to initially put together a comprehensive list of desired characteristics. This can be anything from a person's ability to demonstrate kindness to the way a person grooms their hair. Understanding the specific traits you are looking for in a prospect ahead of time will make the research stage a lot easier. This is because in your research you can assess if the prospect more or less fits into your ideal prospect profile.

In the case of general business, the ideal customer profile (ICP) is a hypothetical description of the type of individual or company that fits your product or service offering while also complementing the traits you are looking for. This can be anything from company size, technologies the company uses, or where the company is located.

There are many ways you can use an ICP in the independent film world. This includes but is not limited to:

- Identifying the best type of distribution company to reach out to that fits your project, using characteristics such as genre, budget levels, attached talent, etc.

- Discovering the best production companies to target for your visual special effects services

- Pointing out an actor or actress to engage with for your project, using characteristics such as physical appearance, age, and work experience

- Locating a screenwriter to option a screenplay from, using characteristics such as a low-budget, limited location screenplay requiring no special effects, children, or animals

Questions to Ask Yourself

Because the point of research is to ensure you are focusing on the prospects who tick all the major boxes, through this process you must ask yourself a series of questions. Some of these potential questions include:

- Does this person have the right qualifications and experience to be a good match for the film project you are working on?

- What kind of resources can this person bring to the project?

- Are they geographically located in a place that makes sense for your potential relationship?

- How long have they been in business and/or practicing their craft?

- Are there any signs this person might not be a good fit for your project or service?

- What film projects has this person or company worked on in the past?

It's important to note that, before proceeding to the next step in the prospecting process, you must run through these qualification questions in order to prioritize your outreach efforts. The last thing you want to do is reach out to someone who is automatically not a good fit for you and waste your time. You want to make sure your prospect is considered "qualified," which means recognized to be a good fit. An "unqualified" prospect is someone who doesn't fit the necessary criteria for the role. Once you have identified a list of prospects who pass your qualification criteria, you are ready to move on to the next prospecting stage.

Step #2: Outreach

In the world of sales, outreach refers to the activity of engaging with prospects or past customers who have either gone cold or may have the potential to become active customers of yours. This engagement can occur in a variety of ways, including some of the communication tools mentioned earlier. Whether it's through email, phone calls, social media, or knocking on their door, the most important goal to achieve out of your outreach is to deliver a message that introduces yourself and your product, provides how you can bring value to them, and ultimately prompts a call-to-action from your prospect.

As an independent filmmaker, your initial outreach will be different when speaking to a film financier compared with that of an actor or a screenwriter. Not only will your messaging be different but the means of communication will differ as well. For example, it would make sense to reach out to an Instagram influencer via Instagram, but it wouldn't make sense to reach out to a film financier through the same medium. Your initial outreach will also differ if the person is a contract worker versus an employee of a large company. Performing outreach to actors can differ depending on if the actor has a manager or agent you must reach out to beforehand. Your desired outcome from your initial outreach is to move to the second stage of the sales process, which is holding a discovery call.

In your initial outreach to a prospect, it's important to use the research you have conducted on them to identify the best outreach channel, overcome call reluctance, personalize your messaging, request the most appropriate call-to-action, and, lastly, build a solid follow-up cadence.

Use the Research You Have Done

With all the hard work you have put into scanning the internet and having conversations with shared connections, now it's time to put this information to good use. Before crafting a well-written email or picking up the phone and dialing a prospect, you want to have a general idea of the research you have conducted on this person. If you read an article about a recent success, you might want to include it in your conversation. You can also use the information you obtained to avoid touching on certain topics. Referrals are always a great way to make a warm introduction. In your email, if you mention you are good friends with Bob and Bob knows them, it will automatically make the prospect feel closer to you. If you researched in an online interview that a director has a passion for war-themed stories, this is something you might want to include in your email to share how you are currently developing a script on the Civil War.

Identify the Best Outreach Channel

Not all communication mediums are created equal. Reaching out to someone via their personal Facebook profile might not be the best course of action in certain situations. Despite the growing popularity of social media over the past few years, it's crucial to note that in order to validate the legitimacy of your project as an independent filmmaker, you must strategize the outreach channel that will relay your professionalism. Showing up to their office with no scheduled appointment can also turn out to be a complete disaster. You need to ask yourself what the most appropriate outreach channel is. What outreach channel you use to reach out to a prospect will vary depending on their preference, what contact information you have available, and the nature of the conversation. It can make sense to walk into a camera rental facility and spark a conversation surrounding the equipment you will need for your shoot. However, it wouldn't be a smart idea to burst into a major distribution company's offices with no appointment.

Overcoming Call Reluctance

This is an occurrence in which an individual will come up with every reason in the world to NOT pick up the phone or send an email. It's an emotional hesitation to prospect and self-promote. This is an experience even the best salespeople struggle with. When you have done your research on a prospect and know your product offering inside and out, you will find that you are more motivated to get in front of people. It's when you lack in preparation by not doing your homework that you will find yourself making every excuse in the book not to pick up the phone. Taking a deep breath and thinking about your most recent business success will help relieve your anxieties. You should also remove any distractions from your physical and digital workspace and even seek guidance from a trusted source of yours. Before sending out an email to a potential financier you were referred to, by doing your homework and discovering they recently invested in a similar film that became a hit, you will be more confident in having a conversation.

Personalize Your Message

Getting the attention from a prospect largely depends on your ability to build trust and differentiate yourself from others. Think about how many people reach out to this person on a daily basis. They have countless conversations with people from all walks of life, including other filmmakers like you. While conducting outreach, customizing your message with your prospect's name and company, along with some context from the research you have done on them will ensure your message will stand out from the rest. Some ways you can personalize your message include using an attention grabbing subject line in your email, asking a unique question highlighting something about their work, mentioning a shared connection, and more. People love receiving recognition from others. In the beginning of your message, if you can incorporate a compliment on one of their recent projects or some other achievement, it will strike a chord and ultimately get their attention.

Request a Call-to-Action

A call-to-action is an invitation for the prospect to take some desired action. Calls-to-action can be found everywhere. You can find them in political campaigns encouraging citizens to register to vote or sign a petition for a social cause. You can also find them while you shop on e-commerce websites, directing you to purchase one of their popular products before it goes out of stock. If you are reaching out to someone who you are not already acquainted with, your goal from your initial outreach should be to introduce yourself and schedule a discovery call to learn more about the prospect and provide insight into your product or service. This casual thirty-minute discovery call can either be an in-person meeting, a phone call, or video conference, depending on what makes sense given your geographic location and schedule. In some instances, you might ask your prospect to review a piece of material before hopping on a discovery call with them. As an independent filmmaker you might use a call-to-action to have a distributor checkout a screener of your film, have an actress read your script, or have a financier look over your business plan before scheduling a meeting to chat about it. The call-to-action is presented toward the end of your outreach communication after you have briefly expressed who you are, why you are reaching out, and what you hope to accomplish by having a discussion.

Build a Follow-up Sequence

Did you know that 80 percent of sales are made on the fifth to twelfth follow-up, and only 2 percent of sales are made on the first contact? The cold hard truth is that, more often than not, people will not respond to the first message you send them. Whether it's a first email or voicemail, your prospect will most likely not respond right away due to lack of time or lack of interest. This is why the initial research you conduct on this person is so important. By taking the time to investigate this person, you are simultaneously collecting ammunition to ensure your prospect completes your call-to-action and engages with you in a discovery call.

Throw Sh*t Against the Wall

One final note on the outreach stage involves massive outreach. For the most part, sales is a numbers game. The more emails you send, the more proposals you present, and the more calls you make, the more likely you will be to close a deal. It's not enough to reach out to one person in hopes that it will result in a sale. You must multiply your movements to increase your odds. For example, instead of reaching out to five companies, reach out to twenty. It's better to be in a position where you are worried about striking too much interest from too many people, as opposed to getting no interest from one person. You never want to put all your eggs in one basket, despite your belief that one person or one company is the ultimate answer.

As an independent filmmaker, it wouldn't make sense to only rely on one potential financier. Nor would it make sense to only reach out to one distribution company or international sales agent. You especially wouldn't depend on one film editor when there are thousands to choose from.

- What if this person or company doesn't get back to you?

- What if they are not interested in your project?

- What if they turn out to be unqualified to work on your project?

In the research stage you should be spending a fair amount of time building an extensive list of similar individuals and companies who serve as a backup to your number one choice. It's fine to have a list of your number one, number two, and your last-place choices, similar to what high school graduates do for college applications.

At this point, if you have effectively conducted your initial outreach to your prospect by introducing yourself, providing insight into your film project, and requesting a call-to-action, your prospect should have seen the value in what you and your project have to offer and will ultimately respond to learn more. Congratulations! You successfully got their attention, and you are ready to move on to the third step of prospecting.

Step #3: Schedule a Discovery Meeting

The formal definition of the word *discovery* is "the act of finding or learning something for the first time." Getting the opportunity to learn something about your prospect is exactly what a discovery meeting is all about. The discovery meeting is the first meeting after connecting with a prospect where both parties learn about each other. This initial meeting sets the tone for the entire relationship and it's crucial to ensure you make a good first impression. In the next section I will be going over what a discovery meeting is in detail. Nevertheless, in the first stage of prospecting your goal is to schedule a discovery meeting. Here are a few tips on how to schedule a successful discovery meeting.

Prioritize Their Schedule

Since you are reaching out to this person to have a conversation surrounding your film project, you want to work within a time window that works best for them. Your prospect is taking a few minutes out of their day to chat with you and you want to make a good first impression by not being selfish and not working within their schedule. Ask what day and time works best for them to join a call. You usually want to book the meeting out a day or two to give the prospect enough time to prepare beforehand. Sometimes it even makes sense to book the discovery meeting out a week or more. For example, when speaking to a potential investor, you want to ensure you have given them enough time to review your business plan and put together any questions or concerns they have. When speaking to an actress, you want to give her enough time to read your script and study the character. It wouldn't make sense to ask to speak to the investor or actress the day after you sent the business plan or screenplay. The chances this person is going to drop everything that day to read your collateral is very slim. Scheduling a meeting a week or two out will indirectly invoke a sense of urgency for your prospect to complete the call-to-action before speaking to you. Whether it's reading your screenplay, reviewing your pitch deck, or watching your director's reel, realistically think about how long it would take this person to finish, and keep in mind: you are not their only priority.

Clarify the Mode of Communication

After your prospect has agreed to a meeting, you need to clarify whether you want to meet in person, do a phone call, or hold a video conference. An in-person meeting is always the best choice because you have the ability to read their nonverbal cues, and it's more efficient when trying to clarify your thoughts. If you live within driving distance of your prospect I would recommend pitching for an in-person meeting if possible. Casually asking to meet at a coffee shop or local restaurant is your best bet because it serves as a middle ground so you and your party won't feel intimidated being in the other person's home court. If a phone call or a video conference makes more sense (because of Covid or other considerations), be sure to inform your prospect on the number you will be calling from, the dial-in code for the video conference, or any other pertinent details. It's way more powerful to deliver an in-person business plan presentation to an investor. It's also easier to express your passion and excitement for one's screenplay when meeting face to face with a writer.

Ask if You Should Invite Any Other Attendees

In some cases it makes sense to ask the prospect if there are any additional people they believe should join the call to learn more about your project, as they might not be the sole decision maker. For example, in some cases when reaching out to an actor, they may feel their manager or agent should be the one you should have an initial conversation with. A financier might have a close associate or friend who also invests in films and may potentially be interested in learning more about your project. After your prospect responds with interest in a meeting, ask if there is anyone else they feel would benefit from joining the conversation before sending out a calendar invite.

Send Out a Calendar Invite

Once you have set a time that works for both you and your prospect, it's time to send out a calendar invite to ensure your prospect remembers the meeting date and time. I recommend using the calendar tool associated with your email account. Gmail and Outlook have great calendar capabilities, allowing a prospect to approve the meeting request and will even provide a reminder ten minutes before the meeting time. The calendar invite title can be straightforward, such as: "Prospect's name and your name or company name: Introduction."

Provide Detail on What the Meeting Will Cover

In the description of the calendar invite you want to include as much detail about what the meeting will cover. This way your prospect will come prepared and will be able to contribute as much as possible. Being clear about what you are going to be talking about will most likely prompt some questions or additional input from the attendees, which will also help in establishing your formal meeting agenda later on. For example, you can explain to an investor you will be providing a high-level overview of your film's pitch deck and business plan. You can send a brief outline to a prospective production manager surrounding your production goals and the major points you want to get across.

Send a Reminder Twenty-Four Hours Before the Meeting

We are all guilty of forgetting a preplanned engagement. Whether it is a lunch with a friend or an important business meeting with a client, we gladly accept the invitation but when the day arrives we forget what we agreed to. We are all humans, and the fact is, things come up! By sending your prospect a friendly and short reminder email twenty-four hours before your appointment, you are increasing the chances your prospect doesn't forget about your discovery call and will ultimately show up. If your prospect needs to reschedule due to an event that popped up, it's better to know ahead of time and commit for another date instead of not having the full attention of your prospect.

A Note on CRMs

A customer relationship management (CRM) tool is a program that helps salespeople streamline the entire sales process by keeping all of their contacts and accounts organized, and tracking all of the communication history they have had with their prospects and customers. Because they are reaching out to a massive number of people, it makes their life easier when they have the ability to look at a high level of all of their activity. CRMs help salespeople in a variety of ways, including centrally housing all of the research they have done, keeping track of conversation history, and seeing what stage they are at with each prospect in the sales process. Some popular CRMs include companies like HubSpot, Salesforce, Zoho, and Close.io.

A CRM would be extremely useful for an independent filmmaker as well. You can record all of the distribution companies and international sales agencies, along with the relevant employees and their contact information. In the notes section of each account you can document the list of films that the distribution company and international sales agent have worked on in the past, along with the types of genres they tend to specialize in. For potential crew members and film equipment companies, you can make notes on their work experience, the type of resources they can provide, and any other relevant information. If you are working with an actress, you can include relevant contacts associated with her, including her publicist, agent, and manager. Emails, phone numbers, physical addresses, and website links are all data you can collect on the prospect's direct website, IMDbPro profile, or any contact paid or unpaid database. It's extremely helpful to have a CRM to record the dates you have met with the person and reminders of what you talked about. Some CRMs even have a Google Chrome plugin, allowing you to sync your email data to each contact so you can easily reference every single email exchange.

Prospecting Summary

As the first stage of the sales cycle, prospecting is a major portion that arms a salesperson with the right ammunition before he or she attacks. Being sure you are reaching out to the right individuals will save you time, energy, and sometimes even money. As you have learned, there are three key areas one must perform in the prospecting phase: research, outreach, and scheduling the discovery meeting.

Researching a prospect's work history, common connections, and the company background or five-minute newspaper interview are all examples of items you might record before reaching out. Talking to a shared acquaintance about how a distributor did a great job on marketing their film might make you realize the company might not be a good fit for you and your goals. Building a customer profile of your ideal cinematographer before you reach out to one, which includes their shot aesthetics, work ethic, and ability to bring their unique vision to the table, will ensure you pick the perfect candidate for the position. Lastly, taking a step back and asking yourself qualifying questions surrounding the prospect is a way to be certain you don't waste your time engaging someone who would never be a good fit.

Being mindful of how you communicate with your prospect is another area of prospecting often overlooked. Sometimes it makes more sense to reach out to them via phone or email, such as in the case of a film director or an actress. Other times it might be okay to show up in person and have a quick chat, such as a camera rental facility, a location you want to shoot at, or a post-production house. Using the research you have done on this person, you can personalize your message to ensure you set yourself apart from all the other proposals they receive on a day-to-day basis. Don't get caught up in your head and reluctantly hesitate to pick up the phone or send them an email. Be confident in what you and your project have to offer this person and demonstrate your conviction and passion. In your outreach make sure you provide your prospect with a call-to-action before asking for the discovery meeting. This can be anything from reviewing a camera and lighting budget to sending a pitch deck centered on potential locations for the film. You want to ensure your prospect has more than enough time to review this material before they meet with you. Because it's very unlikely they will respond to your initial email or voicemail, keep in mind that you are most likely going to need multiple touch points to finally get them to respond to you. Persistence is key.

In conclusion, once your prospect has expressed interest in either meeting with you in person or on a phone call, you must schedule a time to hold a discovery meeting. Prioritizing their schedule, clarifying what communication tool will be used for the discovery meeting, and asking them if they are any other stakeholders whom you should invite to the meeting are all steps to ensure you are on the same page. For example, you might want to ask another producer to meet with you in person at a local coffee shop to create a more casual environment. If you are talking to a caterer, it would make sense to ask if he or she has a partner who would also like to join. Using your email's calendar function, you can send out a formal calendar invite that includes a high-level overview of what the meeting will be about. Sending your prospect a reminder email twenty-four hours before the discovery call will mitigate the risk of your prospect not showing up. With all of these prospects in your pipeline, it can be hard to keep track of everything. Implementing a CRM tool to keep track of your conversation history, contact information, and notes might be a smart idea.

CHAPTER 2
PROSPECTING—A CASE STUDY

Prospecting the Screenwriter

As an independent filmmaker, you are always looking for that ground-breaking story to share with the world. With so many screenwriters out there hustling their storylines, it can be hard to narrow down the perfect fit. I'm sure some of you are thinking you can use your friend's script or write the screenplay yourself. However, what if you are looking to take your career to the next level by optioning a highly recognized screenplay or book? What if writing isn't your strong suit?

As an independent filmmaker you are going to be exposed to a variety of talented writers and being able to discover those writers and screenplays before anyone else will place you at a competitive advantage. Most importantly, not being afraid to reach out to a writer in hopes of working with them will increase your chances of producing or directing outstanding films.

According to *Script Magazine*, there are around two hundred thousand active screenwriters at any given time. Out of the two hundred thousand, two thousand of them are able to write good to great scripts, while another eight thousand are able to put out average screenplays. Therefore, you are looking at about ten thousand writers who are creating innovative stories that can elevate your filmmaking career.

With so many available screenwriters and scripts in this world, how does a filmmaker find that needle in the haystack? When they do find that piece of gold, how does one reach out to a writer and ultimately option it? What kind of research should be done before reaching out, and what should you say when you do finally make contact with this person? It all starts with the first stage of the sales process: prospecting. Let's start with step one of the prospecting phase: research.

Phase 1—Researching the Screenwriter

Before you can conduct any sort of research on any single screen-writer, you must have a general idea of what type of project you are looking to produce. There are so many types of formats, from television shows, to internet series, to feature films. There are also a variety of genres, from horror and fantasy to comedy and action-adventure. Once you have identified the format and the genre of choice, you are ready to proceed to the research phase.

Step #1: Build an Ideal Project and Screenwriter Profile

Now that you have identified the type of format and genre for your next project, you will find that there are thousands of choices when it comes to available screenplays and screenwriters. Because nobody has the time to sift through five thousand scripts, it will make your life a whole lot easier if you specified your project and the type of screenwriter you would ideally like to work with in further detail, by ultimately building ideal profiles for both.

FIGURE 2A   PROJECT: IDEAL PROFILE

Project Format: Feature Film
Genre: Dark Comedy
Budget Level: Ultra-low-budget (700k - 2.5 mil)
Setting: Must take place in the United States in a rural environment
Time Period: Present-Day
# of Locations: Limited locations (fewer than 4) - Must take place on a farm

Continued

# of Main Characters: Fewer than 3 (One of them being a girl between the ages of 18 and 25)
Additional Notes: No special effects/stunts, no actors under the age of 18, no animals, no elaborate sets or rare props, and the screenplay must be longer than 90 pages but shorter than 120 pages.

In Figure 2A, you can see how specific one can be when looking for a project. As a filmmaker you need to realistically take a look at your experience and ask yourself how much money you think you can raise for your project. An independent filmmaker who has recently graduated college and is starting out will most likely be working with a significantly smaller budget than a professional who has been producing films for over a decade. Also ask yourself the type of resources you already have available. In Figure 2A's example, this person has access to a farm in a rural area. They also have access to an actress between the ages of 18 and 25. Lastly, they are set on keeping the project simple by not having any sort of expensive elements such as special effects, underage actors, animal trainers, or any unique film set constructions.

FIGURE 2B   SCREENWRITER: IDEAL PROFILE

Geography: Based in the United States
Union Affiliation: Non-union
Work Experience: At least 5 years of experience
# of scripts produced: 0-2
Budget: Would be willing to option their screenplay or work with me on creating a new screenplay for a maximum of $1,500.
Work Ethic: Someone who is dedicated to their craft and is completely open to constructive criticism. They are always thinking outside the box but at the same time they are very organized in their process. Since I'm looking to move into production by next summer, I'm looking for someone who has enough time to make any necessary adjustments or rewrites.
Potential Goals: This person is talented at what they do but isn't at a point where they can ask for a lot of money for their work or services. Ideally this person should have few to none of their projects produced and are desperately looking to get to the next step of their writing career.

Continued

Additional Notes: Someone who isn't represented by an agent or manager and who has the communication skills to articulate their characters and plot lines. This person must also not be too emotionally attached to their work to the point of constant complaints and distractions during the entire filmmaking process.

In Figure 2B, the filmmaker went even further and created a detailed profile for the type of screenwriter they ideally would like to work with. This filmmaker thought it was important to note that they didn't want to deal with any sort of restrictions or regulations from writers unions like the Writers Guild of America. Nor did they want to deal with any third parties like managers and agents, who might serve as a bottleneck in negotiating a price. Although the filmmaker is going to want to negotiate the lowest possible price for the screenwriter's work, he or she has stated a ceiling of $1,500 to option a script or engage a screenwriter for their services. Lastly, the filmmaker expressed interest in someone with amateur experience but has the work ethic and drive to get one of their screenplays produced for the silver screen. Most importantly, this filmmaker even included personality characteristics that were not of interest in the additional notes section.

After you have completed both the ideal profile for your project and screenwriter, you are ready to start your scavenger hunt for your golden script.

Step #2: Use Online Tools to Find Screenplays and Screenwriters

Now that you have identified high-level criteria of the type of script you are looking for, along with the hopeful characteristics of a screenwriter, you are ready to perform your search. Since we have been living in the Information Age for quite some time, we can take advantage of the internet and all it has to offer.

One type of tool to take advantage of when you are searching for a screenplay is that of online websites that specialize in connecting filmmakers and writers. Some of my personal favorites include:

- **Screenwriting Staffing:** An online staffing tool that connects screenwriters to industry professionals like talent managers, agents, and producers. Whether it's the goal of selling a script or securing a long-term writing assignment, Screenwriting Staffing is built to help connect writers to movers and shakers in the movie industry. For an independent filmmaker, it's free to use and can potentially result in matching you to your all-star writer. Using your Project Ideal Profile (PIP) and your Screenwriter Ideal Profile (SIP), you can perform a detailed screenwriting and screenwriter search. The website also has a Log line Board section where you can check out the log lines of available screenplays for specific genres. Once you fill out the website's form for what you are looking for in a project and screenwriter, Screenwriting Staffing will connect you to a variety of writers that match your criteria.

- **Script Revolution:** Another free script-hosting website that provides writers with a platform to advertise their work and a way for filmmakers to discover them. As of June 2020, with over seven thousand screenplays available and over six thousand users, this platform has a lot to offer. Similar to the capabilities of other screenplay platforms, Script Revolution allows filmmakers to narrow down their search using specific elements like the screenplay's length, time period, theme, special effects, and more. Once you find a script that appears to fit your PIP, you can download it, read it, and easily reach out to the writer if you are interested in pursuing it.

- **Simply Scripts:** With its simple design, Simply Scripts is more than a screenplay database. This website has access to hundreds of thousands of television, film, musical, and theater scripts, both produced and unproduced. In the unproduced section of the website, you can find a list of genres ranging from psychological thrillers to comedies. Unfortunately, this website doesn't have the high-level search functionality that other screenplay hosting sites have. However, there are plenty of options to choose from, and it will cost you nothing. When you find a log line that grabs

your attention, you can click on the title to access the PDF version of the script. If you want to contact the writer, all you have
to do is click on the writer's name to access their email address.

- **InkTip:** Originated in 2000, Inktip.com is an online platform
that connects producers and screenwriters. Saving you time and
money, Inktip connects independent producers to a library of
thousands of available screenplays for option or purchase. In order to create an account as a producer, you must fit their qualifications, which include industry references, previous film credits,
background in the industry, and any other relevant information
that gives them insight into your experience as a filmmaker. Once
you are approved, you are given access to a thorough database
of available scripts, which you can narrow down by specific elements. For example, using your Project Ideal Profile (PIP), you
can do a search query to match a certain genre, budget range,
location count, and more. Once you find a script that closely
matches your search criteria, you can download a PDF version
to read. The contact information of the writer is also available.

- **The Black List:** Developed in 2005, The Black List is another
online platform that connects producers to top writing talent.
The website started out as an internal Hollywood list of the best
screenplays that have been floated around town but has grown
into more in the past few years. In order to gain access to the
website you must qualify for an industry membership, which
will require you to share information like your IMDb link and
any notable industry references that can vouch for you. If you
have a connection that works at a major talent agency, such as
William Morris Endeavor or Creative Artists Agency, your best
bet is to reach out to them to be your referral. Given the high
number of executives from major studios, talent agencies, and
management firms, The Black List is on the more elite scale of
screenplay databases in my opinion. Once you do gain access
to the platform, you will find that you can use search filters to
easily pin down your PIP. Once you find a script that gets your
attention, you can read it on the website's platform or easily save

it to your computer. The contact information for the writer will also be available and you will find that other readers' reviews on the script are very helpful.

After reading an array of screenplays from the above resources, at this point you should have a few narrowed down. Before you can reach out to any of the screenwriters, you want to make sure that you do a quick internet search of their name and see what comes up.

Step #3: Screenwriter Research

You are now at the part of the first step where you can conduct research on your prospective screenwriter. This is a very important step that you do not want to overlook as this will aid you in collecting the right ammunition before your outreach.

Using the key research areas in the previous chapter, in Figure 2C you can see a hypothetical example of what this precise research would look like for a screenwriter.

FIGURE 2C   SCREENWRITER RESEARCH

Work Experience/LinkedIn: After performing a Google search of this person's name, I came across their LinkedIn profile, which shows she is based in Austin, Texas, and is a full-time executive assistant for an e-commerce website that I happen to frequently shop from. It appears that she has been with the company for over ten years and that she obtained her college education at New York University, which happens to be where I also attended school. There are no other previous jobs listed except a part-time screenwriting role. It says that she has written over five screenplays the past four years. However, it doesn't appear that any of these screenplays were made into actual films.

Notable Connections: Since we both attended New York University, we have six shared connections on LinkedIn, one of them being one of my close friends from college, Andrew. I frequently speak to Andrew, and it wouldn't be an "out of the ballpark" idea to reach out to him and ask him if he can tell me something about her. Or possibly even introduce me to her if it makes sense.

Continued

Company Background: It says she works for the e-commerce website OnlineShop, which happens to be one of my favorite places to purchase my home goods. I also found a link to her screenwriting portfolio website where she lists a mission statement to "connect audiences to ground-breaking stories that will entertain them while also making them think differently about the world they live in."

Media Attention: There weren't many news articles or much publicity surrounding her screenwriting. The only thing I can find is a link to a recent screenwriting competition based in Los Angeles that lists her and the name of one of her other screenplays as the second-place winner. The award was for "Best Written" screenplay, and it appears that there were 3,500 submissions.

After conducting the above research, which can possibly take any-where from a few minutes to a few hours, depending on how much information there is out there about this person, you can summarize the major points from your discoveries, shown in Figure 2D.

FIGURE 2D   SCREENWRITER RESEARCH SUMMARY

- Found her dark comedy screenplay CHASERS on Screenwriting Staffing
- Currently based in Austin, Texas
- Went to college at NYU and graduated five years before me
- Works full-time as an executive assistant at the e-commerce website OnlineShop and has been with the company for ten years
- Has worked part-time as a screenwriter for the past 4 years and has written over 5 screenplays
- We share 6 connections on LinkedIn, which includes my good college friend Andrew
- She won second place in a recent Los Angeles–based screenwriting competition that had over 3,500 submissions

By summarizing your research in a concise one-page format, you are making it easier to see the high-level facts and shared connections. One final note is to use this high-level summary and look at the ISP you created on your screenwriter. Does this person match the number of years of experience? Does it appear he or she will have enough time to work on script edits and notes? Have any of their screenplays been produced before? All of these elements will be extremely useful for you when you are drafting your initial outreach email.

Phase 2—Screenwriter Outreach

Now is the time to use the research you have done on both the script and the writer and craft a well-articulated message expressing your desire to have a productive conversation with this person surrounding their screenplay. Even if you don't use all of the research you found in your initial outreach, who is to say you might not use it during the discovery call or at some other point in the future.

Constructing the solid outreach with the goal of connecting with your screenwriter can be broken down into multiple steps as follows:

Step #1: Identify Best Outreach Channel

When you are dealing with someone you have never met, it makes sense why one would be hesitant to introduce themself in person or over the phone if they also have the ability to email them. Although in-person and phone connect are always the better options, for the sake of this hypothetical case study I will use email as the best initial outreach channel. In scenarios where you have prior engagement with the prospect, whether it be via a third-party connection or a shared lunch place, it's more acceptable to pick up the phone and give them a call or directly walk up to them and introduce yourself.

For our hypothetical case study, our independent filmmaker located the screenwriter's direct email on the Screenwriting Staffing website.

Step #2: Introduce Yourself and Personalize Your Message

Since we are using email as the medium of communication, you are going to want to first introduce yourself and provide insight on why you are reaching out to them in the first place. The first thing to pay attention to is your subject line. You want it to be clear on why you are reaching out while also not coming off tacky.

FIGURE 2E SCREENWRITING OUTREACH - SUBJECT LINE AND INTRODUCTION

Subject Line: Introduction | Read your script "Chasers"

Hi Janice,

My name is Alec, and I recently came across your screenplay on Screenwriting Staffing. I wanted to start off by saying that I am a huge fan of your writing style and I enjoyed reading CHASERS. You have quite the talent in dark comedies, which explains why you were a finalist in a national screenplay competition that had over 3,500 submissions. Congratulations!

To give you background on myself, I'm an independent filmmaker based out of Los Angeles. My company is Coast ART Productions. Some of our titles include the international feature film THE CABIN (2018), the short subject drama TOO FAR FROM HOME (2013), and an upcoming romantic comedy, OLD MAN DESPERADO (2021).

In Figure 2E you can see I used a very basic subject line articulating my intentions. I want to introduce myself and have a conversation surrounding her screenplay. I did this because I want to avoid any sort of confusion and mitigate the risk of her deleting my email and marking it as spam. In the beginning of my email, I tell her who I am and how I found her. These are usually the first two things people want to know when being contacted: *Who is this person? And how did they find me?*

By providing praise on her work and even including some of the high-level research I have done on her to congratulate her, I'm starting off the email in a way that would make any reader smile. People love to be complimented, and it's a surefire way to get someone's attention to want to learn more.

Lastly, I provide a few sentences on my background and work experience. This doesn't need to be very long, since the aim is to go further in detail over the phone. Stating you are an independent filmmaker and listing any relevant projects you have worked on in the past will build a sense of initial credibility. If you do not have any projects in your portfolio, it's important to be honest and share your objective of making your first film.

Step #3: Request a Call-to-Action

With a strong subject line and clear introduction consisting of a personalized message demonstrating the research you did, you most likely have your prospect's full attention. Now it's time for the next step of your outreach, which is requesting a call-to-action.

Although your ultimate goal is to option her screenplay and produce it, you don't want to show all of your cards outright. It's like telling a girl you newly met that you want to marry her or a car dealer you that want to purchase a specific car and you don't care how much it costs.

FIGURE 2F   SCREENWRITER OUTREACH - CALL TO ACTION

I wanted to schedule time this week to hop on an introductory call to learn more about your writing background and goals and any relevant developments related to CHASERS. I'm looking to produce my next feature film, and I would like to throw around a few ideas with you.

Let me know what day and time works best for you. Looking forward to chatting!

Best,
Alec Trachtenberg

The second half of my email, Figure 2F, shows you my request to hop on an introductory call to discuss her background and developments with the screenplay I am ultimately interested in optioning. However, instead of coming off too aggressive, I'm politely asking to have a casual conversation to talk about her writing and goals. If someone has the opportunity to share their goals with someone who might be able to help them out, they would sign up in a heartbeat. By saying you are in the process of searching for your next feature, you are allowing her to connect the dots on how her script might be a potential option.

Lastly, to increase your chances of a desired result from your prospect, you must be confident and use language that assumes the other person is on board with what you are saying. By asking what day and time works for her, I'm not only being cordial of her availability but I am also concluding she has already agreed to meet with me. Telling her I look forward to chatting with her is the icing on the cake.

FIGURE 2G   SCREENWRITER OUTREACH - EXAMPLE

Subject Line: Introduction | Read your script "Chasers"

Hi Janice,

My name is Alec and I recently came across your screenplay on Screenwriting Staffing. I wanted to start off by saying that I am a huge fan of your writing style and I enjoyed reading CHASERS. You have quite the talent in dark comedies, which explains why you were a finalist in a national Screenplay competition that had over 3,500 submissions. Congratulations!

To give you a little background on myself, I'm an independent filmmaker based out of Los Angeles. My company is Coast ART Productions. Some of our titles include the international feature film THE CABIN (2018), the short subject drama TOO FAR FROM HOME (2013), and an upcoming romantic comedy, OLD MAN DESPERADO (2021).

I wanted to schedule time this week to hop on an introductory call to learn more about your writing background and goals and any relevant developments related to CHASERS. I'm looking to produce my next feature film, and I would like to throw around ideas with you.

Let me know what day and time works best for you. Looking forward to chatting!

Best,
Alec Trachtenberg

Step #4: Build a Follow-up Sequence

Given that most writers would be extremely excited to hear that someone enjoyed their work and has even gone a step further to compliment them and request a conversation to talk about their writing background and goals, there is the slim chance you might have to send a follow-up email or two.

Luckily, all of the main points are addressed in your initial email, so your follow-up emails do not have to be very comprehensive. The goal of the follow-up is for your initial message to resurface to the top of your prospect's inbox. Strange things happen on a daily basis, and sometimes people forget to respond. Sometimes your message might have been hidden in your prospect's spam folder. Despite the many possible reasons as to why your prospect hasn't responded, it's important to send a follow-up at least 3 to 5 days after sending your initial message. As a general rule, you should send a follow-up email every 3 to 5 days if still no response. If the screenwriter's phone number is listed, it might make sense to pick up the phone and give them a call if you haven't heard back after the second or third email.

FIGURE 2H   SCREENWRITER FOLLOW-UP - EXAMPLE

Hi Janice,

Not sure if you received my previous email from a few days ago. With SXSW happening right now in Austin, I'm sure you are probably very busy!

To reiterate my last message, I would like to schedule time to hop on a call to discuss your screenplay CHASERS and to chat with you surrounding your writing experience and your initiatives for the project.

What does your schedule look like either Thursday or Friday afternoon? Let me know what day and time works best for you, and I'll send over a calendar invite.

Best,
Alec

In Figure 2H, you can see how I strategically used more of the research I have done on my prospect to express my interest and knowledge of her background and to set myself apart from the other generic emails she gets on a daily basis. I proceed to summarize my last email and explain my desire to chat with her about her experience and her goals for *Chasers*.

Putting yourself in their shoes, you can only imagine the time and energy they spent working on their screenplay. Expressing interest in learning about what they have in mind for the project will set you apart from so many other filmmakers who don't stop to think about asking what the writer's aspirations are before going into what the filmmaker wants to accomplish. It's important the writer gets the sense you are genuinely looking out for their best interest. A psychiatrist wouldn't prescribe a patient medication without finding out what's wrong with them first, right? The same thing goes for producing a film. A budding filmmaker can't get his option agreement signed by the writer until they uncover what the writer is looking for in the relationship.

At this point the screenwriter should have either responded to your emails or gone dark. As I mentioned in the previous chapter, it's important that you adopt a mentality of massive movements. If one person doesn't get back to you, it doesn't mean everyone else won't. Although you may have fallen in love with the script, it's important to have backup options in place. With your heartfelt compliments, brief but powerful introduction and your influential call-to-action, your prospect has decided to meet with you for an introductory discovery call.

Phase 3—Screenwriter Discovery Meeting

Now it's time to collect all additional relevant information you may need before holding the discovery call, create the calendar invite, and send a reminder email twenty-four hours before the call.

Step #1: Clarify Mode of Communication and Attendee List

After your prospect responds, you must first narrow down a meeting day and time that works for both parties based on their feedback. Keeping in mind where your prospect lives, you can use your best judgment to request either an in-person meeting, a video conference, or a simple phone call. Clarifying the discovery meeting's mode of communication will consist of providing your prospect with the appropriate dial-in information or physical address. For our hypothetical case study, we will go with a standard phone call.

You also want to inquire about any other potential attendees the prospect feels should be included. In the case of a screenwriter, it might make sense to ask them if they have a manager or literary agent they feel should join the call. They might even have a writing partner on the project. If a screenwriter responds with interest in a meeting but doesn't mention their manager or literary agent, I would recommend that it's best not to ask about them. Speaking directly to the decision maker and avoiding interactions with possible barricades is the path to least resistance. However, I have included the attendee clarification in Figure 2J.

FIGURE 2J   SCREENWRITER COMMUNICATION AND ATTENDEE CLARIFICATION - EXAMPLE

Hi Janice,

Wednesday, June 24, at 11:00 am PST works for me! Before I go ahead and send you a calendar invite, I wanted to clarify that we will be speaking over the phone. What is the best number to reach you at that time?

I also wanted to clarify if there were any other individuals you feel should join the call as well? If so, what is their email address so I can also add them on the calendar invitation.

Looking forward to speaking with you in a few days!

Best,
Alec

Step #2: Create the Calendar Invite

After you send your communication and attendee clarification response and receive word from your prospect with answers to your questions, you are ready to set up your calendar invite. Like the subject line of your initial email, you want to keep it simple and straightforward. I like to keep it simple by using the invitation title "Person's Full Name and My Company Name: Introduction."

Using your email account calendar tool, proceed to make a calendar invitation for the specified date the prospect has confirmed, as shown in Figure 2K.

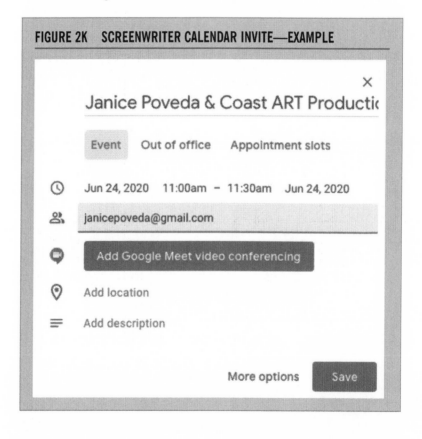

FIGURE 2K   SCREENWRITER CALENDAR INVITE—EXAMPLE

Step #3: Provide Meeting Description

To ensure your screenwriter comes fully prepared and doesn't feel blindsided about what you will be covering during the discovery meeting, it's useful to implement the description section of your calendar invitation.

By no means do you need to express a comprehensive breakdown on every point you hope to discuss during the call. The information you place in this description section should be very high level. Anything from five to ten bullet points. Nothing more.

Lastly, in the location section of the calendar invite be sure to include the number you will be calling the prospect from at the time of the meeting, along with the phone number they advised you to call.

FIGURE 2L   SCREENWRITER CALENDAR INVITE - MEETING DESCRIPTION - EXAMPLE

Hi Janice,

Looking forward to chatting with you on **Wednesday at 11:00 am PST**. To clarify, we will be going over the following during our meeting:

1. Introductions
2. My feedback on CHASERS
   a. Plot structure
   b. Characters
   c. Dialogue
   d. Other comments
3. Your goals and objectives
   a. Screenwriting goals
   b. Goals for CHASERS script
   c. Other project goals
4. Project availability and next steps

Best,
Alec

Step #4: Send a Reminder Email Twenty-Four Hours in Advance

If you scheduled the call for the next day, you most likely don't have to send a reminder email, since you have already communicated fairly close to the meeting time. However, in most cases if you are booking a meeting multiple days or even multiple weeks in advance, you want to send out a meeting reminder to mitigate the risk of your prospect not showing up.

This reminder doesn't need to be too formal. In fact, the more casual the better. One or two sentences about how you look forward to chatting with them regarding their screenwriting background and goals, along with their script, is enough to jog someone's memory on why they agreed to have a call with you in the first place.

FIGURE 2M   SCREENWRITER REMINDER EMAIL - EXAMPLE

Hi Janice,

Hope you're doing well! I wanted to send you a reminder of our sched-uled meeting for tomorrow, **Wednesday, June 24, at 11:00 am PST.** I will be giving you a call on the number you advised, (512) - XXX- XXXX.

Looking forward to chatting about CHASERS and your writing goals!

Best,
Alec

Case Study—A Final Word on Prospecting

Anyone will tell you screenwriting is an important piece of the inde-pendent filmmaking puzzle. By doing the necessary groundwork of putting together your IPP and ISP, you are indirectly making your life easier by identifying realistic criteria for your next film project. It makes more sense for you to have these standards out-lined ahead of time so you don't find yourself spinning your wheels later on in the process. Once you have these standards in place for both your project and your screenwriter, you can proceed to the prospecting stage.

When it comes to prospecting, the important lesson to learn, whether you are dealing with a screenwriter, a financier, or a video-effects artist, is that you must be sure to conduct your initial research on them, create personalized and straight-to-the-point outreach, and correctly set up the meeting invitation. Regardless of what your goal is for this conversation—whether it's optioning a screenplay, getting funding for your film, or purchasing a camera package—you don't want to come off too strong and risk your bargaining hand by immediately telling them your intentions and goals. By asking to jump on an introductory discovery call, you are opening up the conversation to build a long-term relationship and learn more about their goals. When the time comes to negotiate for the screenplay option, camera package, or shooting location, you'll have more information on your prospect to work with to land you a better deal.

STAGE II

DISCOVERY

CHAPTER 3

DISCOVERY

Defining Discovery

At this point in the sales process you have already prospected your candidate by using research and the initial outreach methods outlined in the previous chapters. You have requested to meet with them to introduce yourself and learn more about their goals. The discovery phase is exactly that. It's the process where a salesperson qualifies a prospect and uncovers their objectives. It's also a time where the prospect discovers more about the salesperson and what their offerings can bring to the table.

As the second stage in the sales process, discovery is a two-way conversation aimed at building a positive business relationship. Before you can sell an individual on your project, service, or idea, both parties must first introduce themselves and learn about each other's hopes and plans.

Discovery Goals

Discovery is one of the important stages in the sales process to make certain you are:

■ Building rapport and establishing a relationship with your prospect

- Unearthing your prospect's pain points and personal goals
- Vetting your prospect to ensure they are a good fit for your project or service

Discovery Steps

There are three main steps in the sales discovery process: planning the meeting through research and agendas, leading the call by building a vision as a response to your prospect's pain points and goals, and scheduling next steps to move you one step closer to striking a deal.

Step #1: Plan Your Discovery

You scavenged the entire internet and borderline stalked this person, reached out to any shared connections, and you succeeded in getting the prospect to respond to your outreach. They have accepted a call with you, and the last thing you want to do is come unprepared. It will not only make your prospect feel like he or she is wasting their time, it will make you look unprofessional.

Planning a discovery call consists of building a list of thoughtful questions that can't be answered by a simple Google search. It also consists of creating a call agenda that keeps the conversation on track. These techniques will guarantee a productive meeting that leads to not only a closed deal, but also a prosperous business relationship.

On the chance you get a meeting with a high-profile actress and her agent after sending them your script, the last thing you want to do is look like an amateur by not taking the time to build a list of thought-provoking questions. If you finally get on the phone with a sought-after distribution company but have no plan on how you are going to convincingly pitch your project, wouldn't your prospect feel like you are wasting their time? Lastly, through your research and preparation, if you were able to find out that a financier has a track record of investing in feature films centered on LGBTQIA+ rights, wouldn't it make sense to strategize how you are going to match his initiatives with your project ahead of time?

Create a List of Discovery Questions

Creating thought-provoking questions designed to uncover more than surface-level information is considered an art form. In order for a prospect to feel comfortable revealing their own personal motivations and challenges, you must ask a series of exploratory questions, requiring the prospect to internalize the deeper reason behind their ambitions. The secret is to guide your prospect in a consultative way, sort of like how a doctor would ask a patient questions before being able to diagnose a disease or prescribe a treatment.

The most successful salespeople hold discovery calls centered on the hopes, fears, and work to be done by the prospect, and never only as a place to pitch another one of their products. The questions they ask is the method of making their prospect feel comfortable enough to share.

How to Ask Great Questions

There are a variety of tips and tricks on how to ask great questions. There are thousands of books written on the topic as well. I find the following pointers are the most important to keep top of mind:

- **Plan Your Questions:** Using the research you have done on your prospect coupled with your personal objective of having a conversation, you should have a good idea on what you want to cover on your call. The first thing you want to ask yourself is what your goal is. The questions you put together should all work together to get you closer to your goal. Holding a brainstorming session (either by yourself or with others), writing a list of potential questions on notecards, and referring to areas of the research you did on your prospect are all techniques you can perform to ensure you are coming up with creative and engaging questions. For example, when speaking to an international sales agent, you need to first identify your goal, which is to land a representative who will market your film internationally and outside the United States. Think about all the important questions you would want answers to when it comes to marketing your film to international distributors. Researching "questions to ask an international sales agent" on Google might provide a healthy list of ideas. In addition, by taking the research you have done on this international sales agent, you can ask them about specific projects they have worked on in the past.

- **Don't Ask Yes–No Questions:** As a salesperson you want to keep the conversation natural and flowing. By asking yes–no questions, you will most often get incomplete answers that don't provide you with much to work with. Instead, a salesperson should ask open-ended questions. With open-ended questions you gain insights and even more information because your prospect will provide you with a complete answer. It invites the prospect to talk further and not respond with a short reply. Questions that start with the words "should," "would," "is," "are," and "do you believe" all lead to a yes or no answer. However, starting questions with "who," "how," "what," "when," and "why" will result in your prospect giving some more thought to their responses, ultimately resulting in more discovery for you as a salesperson.

- **Dig Deeper:** By following up with specific questions after asking a general question, you are ensuring you are getting the full picture. Building a hierarchy of questions that begins with general topics will allow you to stay organized in your question asking. Sometimes a prospect's answer will come up short; he or she may assume you know what they are talking about. Asking them to clarify one step further will result in them uncovering more about their true feelings. For example, if you were to ask an actress to tell you about her favorite project she's worked on and followed up by asking her why it was her favorite project, you can potentially uncover a piece of information that will allow you to connect the value proposition of your project.

■ **Use Neutral Wording:** If you want to uncover what your prospect's viewpoints are on certain subject matter, the last thing you
want to do is ask leading questions. A leading question is a question prompting or encouraging a desired answer. For example,
"You would rather work on a comedy next, right?" insinuates
the prospect is more of a fan of the comedy genre over all other
types of films. By asking questions like this you are not letting
your prospect share their feelings. A better question to elicit an
honest response would be: "What genre are you looking forward
to working on next?"

Build a Bullet-Proof Call Agenda

A military general would never let his troops go out to battle without a strategy in place. By the same token, a defense lawyer would
not have any chance of defending his client without a plan of action.
And a successful salesperson would never attend a discovery meeting without a call agenda.

Meetings need an agenda in order to move things along efficiently.
Whether it's a one-on-one meeting or a meeting with a dozen attendees, it's important that all parties are on the same page. Meeting agendas are only necessary if you are the one commencing the meeting.
If the other person reached out to you regarding a job opportunity
on their film project, they would be in charge of leading the meeting.
The last thing you want is any sort of confusion from your meeting
attendees, ultimately costing you the ability to effectively perform
your discovery on them. Here are some important tips to keep in
mind when creating your meeting agenda:

■ **Put together an outline of all possible topics:** After brainstorming all of the potential questions you would like to ask
your prospect, you can identify common themes and ultimately group them into main areas. For example, when formulating
questions for a screenwriter, some of the questions might have to
do with some of their past projects, while some focus on a specific screenplay you read. If you are a cinematographer speaking

to a director, you can ask about their favorite shooting style. When outlining your call agenda, you can establish two topics of conversation, one being the past projects the writer has worked on, and the other on their screenplay.

- **Determine the length of each topic:** Most discovery calls are usually anywhere from thirty to sixty minutes, depending on the nature of the conversation and what's being discussed. Because you don't have time to dive deep into every single topic you created from your list of questions, you must ask yourself what topics warrant more time and attention. When speaking to a potential investor, it doesn't make sense to spend a majority of your time talking about their achievements, risking you not being able to pitch your project for their investment consideration. Although it's important to allow your prospect to feel good about what they have accomplished, you don't want it taking up too much real estate on your call.

- **Communicate your agenda with a strong opener:** In order to set the tone of the meeting, it's imperative you refrain from selling them on your project or services right away. These types of calls are not meant to try to get your prospect to sign the dotted line right away. This is a two-way process, and both parties should aim to build a relationship and contribute valuable information. In the beginning of your call, you want to first thank them for their time and outline what they can expect from the call, the high-level topics on your discovery call agenda. Proceed in asking questions from your list but be sure to have a casual flow. You don't want to come off like you are interrogating your prospect.

Doing your homework before a discovery meeting will set you up to have a productive and insightful conversation with your prospect. With your goal of starting the relationship off on the right foot, asking the right questions, building a call agenda, and connecting your project's or service's value proposition, you will ensure that you uncover an opportunity that makes sense for both parties. Planning will ensure you are successfully able to perform the next step of the discovery process, unearthing and intensifying goals and pain points.

Step #2: Leading Your Discovery

Before you arrive at your meeting or dial their number, it's important to take a deep breath. You should feel confident you are going to win your prospect over with all the preliminary research and work you have conducted up until this point.

Start the conversation by thanking your prospect for joining the meeting. Take everything you have learned about this person and come up with initial friendly questions to set the stage. For example, if the person is based in New York City, you can ask them how the weather is at the moment. If it shows on IMDb that they are currently working on an HBO television series, ask them how everything has been going with the production. The last thing you want to do is nervously rush right into your list of questions and make it seem like a police interrogation.

Leading your discovery call consists of key areas that contribute to a harmonious relationship. Some of these areas include building a sense of rapport, unearthing pain points and goals, using listening techniques, and building a vision of your project or service.

Building Rapport

As an independent filmmaker, you are constantly working with other people from all walks of life. Since we are all in the business of people, wouldn't it make sense to find ways to relate with others? The act of building rapport with another person is exactly that. Rapport building is the initial step in finding common ground—building trust from another person with the goal of making others feel comfortable. Whether you are trying to form a romantic, platonic, or business relationship, it all starts out with rapport building.

Here are a few ways you can initially build rapport with your prospect:

- **Check Your Appearance:** There's no doubt first impressions make a huge impact. The first five seconds with someone can determine how a relationship can evolve. The clothes you wear and the way you groom yourself contributes to how another person can perceive you. If you are meeting with your prospect in person or over video conference, it's important to pay attention to the way you look. Sometimes being overdressed is as bad as being underdressed. Before your meeting assess what you should wear by taking into account the meeting's location and the types of people who will be attending. If you are meeting an executive producer at his production office, it would make more sense to dress professionally than if you are meeting with a cinematographer at a coffee shop. Don't wear anything that can potentially be deemed inappropriate or offensive to your prospect.

- **Mirror and Match:** There are countless studies that conclude people prefer to be around others who they perceive to be like themselves. Psychologist Albert Mehrabian has discovered the words we speak only account for 7 percent of our communication regarding attitudes and emotions. And while the nature of our voice makes up 38 percent, our body language makes up a staggering 55 percent. When it comes to building rapport, watching the other person's body language, posture, and expressions and subtly mirroring them will make the other person feel closer to you. If you notice the person speaks in a quieter tone or at a faster speed, make sure to match it. For example, if you are speaking to a fast-paced producer from New York who wants to get down to talking about your proposed editing services, be sure to match his style and complete his request. On the other hand, if you are speaking to a slow-talking financier who wants to take their time walking through one specific area of your business plan, it would be in your best interest to follow their lead if you want to win them over.

- **Ask General Opening Questions:** These questions should be lighthearted and fun and should be asked at the beginning of the conversation. They serve the purpose of getting your prospect talking right away to make it easier for you to learn more about them. By asking open-ended questions like "What are you looking forward to this weekend?" or "What have you been working on today?" you are inviting your prospect to put down their wall and make themself comfortable talking to you. Because your goal is to eventually get your prospect to share what's keeping them up at night in terms of business problems and some of the goals they have set, the general questions you start with contribute to setting the stage. For instance, if a producer is overlooking your suite of music services and you find out that they've already finished shooting their movie, you can ask them what their favorite part of the shoot was. You want to ask questions that will solicit a positive response to ensure your prospect is in a happy state of mind. If they are in a negative mood, it will be harder for them to let their guard down to share what's on their mind.

- **Find Common Ground:** People love talking about themselves, and the more genuine interest you show in them, the more likely they are to let you in. Perhaps in your research you realize this person went to the same college as you or lived in the same area in the past. Maybe they have worked with someone you know. Through your initial research you will most likely be able to find some common ground. However, you don't want to come off creepy. Paying attention to your tone and how you strategically mention a shared bond will ensure your prospect isn't put off. Remember to also never use their social media as a resource to identify something they have in common with you. Telling a director you also visited the same all-inclusive Mexican resort pictured on his Instagram will not score you any sort of brownie points. Nor would communicating any sort of common ground that can be perceived to be negative. For instance, if you realize both of you have worked with the same person in the past and you both harbor negative feelings about them, it's not in your best interest to talk negatively about this person. This is because it can potentially make you look unprofessional.

- **Make Them Laugh:** Laughter is the best form of medicine. Laughter has been shown to ease anxiety and tension, relax your muscles, boost immunity, and even helps prevent heart disease! The social benefits of laughter include diffusing conflict, promoting group bonding, and ultimately strengthening relationships. When it comes to building rapport with your prospect, telling a joke or sharing a funny story will make them feel comfortable. Reminding others you are human too and not some faceless robot will make your call more casual and enjoyable. People will look forward to talking and doing business with you because they know they can relate to you on more than a business level. Some potential ideas on how to make your prospect laugh include telling a funny story about something that happened to you during a project you've worked on in the past, or sharing a comedic scene out of a movie they might find entertaining. Have a list of funny stories in your back pocket in case you ever need to use it.

- **Know When to Pivot to Business Talk:** The first three to ten minutes of your conversation should be focused on rapport building and light introductions. You don't want to spend too much time building rapport or else you will never get to the meat of the conversation. By mirroring and matching your prospect's communication style, you should be cognizant of the way your prospect is reacting. Usually when the chit-chat dies down and there is a second or two of silence, it's time to bring up the agenda of the discovery call. At this point, you should quickly thank them again for joining the call and provide a concise breakdown on the topics you want to discuss and what you hope to achieve from having the conversation. When speaking with an actress, for example, you can swiftly review the topics of her resume and background, her goals as an actress, and the role in your project you have in mind for her to play. You can mention you hope to learn more about her and see if your project and the character would be a good fit for her.

Unearthing and Intensifying Goals and Pain Points

We all have things that either keep us up at night or keep us motivated. Everyone experiences pain in different ways, but oftentimes we don't know how to articulate what the pain is. This can be anything from teamwork conflicts, inefficient processes, or a lack of sufficient budget. As a salesperson, one of your key assignments is to be able to help your prospect realize they have a problem and ultimately convince them your project or service will help solve it. The same task holds true for your prospects goals. Asking your prospect what their goals are will later allow you to find connections with your offering.

The questions you ask will aid you in the process of unearthing and intensifying goals and pain points. Try asking your prospect questions like "What is the biggest challenge you are facing?", "What takes up most of your day?", and "What area do you need the most help in?". As your prospect provides you with more information, you will be able to paint a clearer picture of what their goals and roadblocks are.

Types of Pain Points

- **Financial:** They are spending too much money and want to reduce the amount they are spending (e.g., a producer working within a limited budget).

- **Productivity:** Your prospect feels like he or she is wasting too much of their time and wants to use their time and resources more efficiently (e.g., a casting director holding a casting call for thousands of actors).

- **Support:** They are not receiving an adequate amount of support from others, whether it's the support from others or technology (e.g., a director not having enough support in the art department).

- **Process:** Your prospect's workflow is inefficient and needs to be improved in some way (e.g., an assistant director experiencing trouble in putting together an effective shooting schedule).

Goals are also ideas prospects are heavily focused on. Goals inspire us, increase our success rate, and genuinely make us happy and fulfilled. The objectives we set for ourselves amplify our identities and what we aim to achieve in all areas of life. Whether it's your career, relationships, money, or health, goals push us to be our best selves.

Types of Goals

- **Outcome:** Specific goals that spell out the result you hope to achieve in the end. Outcome goals are usually compared with one's performance or one's competitor (e.g., the amount of money an independent film makes on VOD).

- **Process:** Goals that follow the behaviors or the strategies that will aid us in performing well and increasing our chances of achieving our objectives. Process goals are within our control and help us achieve our overarching mission (e.g., a screenwriter who has committed to writing every day for the next five days).

- **Performance:** These types of goals set the degree of excellence in how well we perform our process goals. They are the results you produce from your process goals (e.g., a producer who has committed to scheduling five weekly investor calls to pitch his feature film).

The Art of Listening

At this point in the show, you have your prospect in a vulnerable position because you have uncovered their issues and objectives. You need to signal to them you are trustworthy and you are listening. Asking the right questions is one technique you can use. However, being sure to closely listen to what your prospect is saying is another technique that will ensure you get the full breakdown of their problems and initiatives.

Here are some general tips on how to listen to your prospect more effectively:

- **Consistent Eye Contact and Nodding:** Body language plays a huge role in how to communicate with others. Naturally gazing at your prospect while he or she is talking will express that you are listening to them. Be sure you do not stare at them for too long or else it may come off as unsettling. Nodding your head up and down will establish you are interested and fully understand what they are saying to you.

- **Listen to Understand:** Oftentimes people act like they are listening to show they are being polite to the person speaking.

However, listening to be polite is not enough. You need to take it one step further and be genuinely interested in what your prospect has to say. Bringing an authentic desire to listen to your prospect will help make them feel comfortable sharing what's on their mind. Everyone likes to know they are being heard and understood. Listening with a sense of curiosity will achieve exactly that.

Quiet Your Mind: How many thoughts do you think run through your mind on a daily basis? If you are like every other human being, the answer is too many. Experts have found that we have anywhere between 60,000 and 80,000 thoughts cross our mind on a daily basis. When asking questions to prospects, most salespeople are so focused on the questions they ask, they miss the answers the prospect responds with. The gold is found in the answers, not the questions. Silence your mind and try to pay attention to the answers you receive.

- **Be Aware of Your Talk-To-Listen Ratio:** Don't be that person who spends an entire meeting talking the other person's ear off. Since the main goal of the discovery call is to learn about your prospect, the way you are going to achieve this is by letting them talk. You of course want to have time to communicate who you are and what you can bring to the table; however, the spotlight should be on them. Being fully cognizant of how much talking you are doing versus them will ensure you take a step back if needed.

- **Repeat What You Hear:** Parrots do it all the time. Active listening is the act of repeating back to the speaker what you heard. By paraphrasing what your prospect has said, it will demonstrate your understanding. If for some reason there was a miscommunication in what your prospect has said, this will allow them to reword their statement to be clearer to the listener.

Build a Vision

At this point in the discovery meeting, you have uncovered what is important to your prospect. You have asked thoughtful questions and have actively listened. They have shared some knowledge on what is holding them back and what they want to achieve. With this information, you're now ready to build a vision on how your project or service is the answer to their prayers.

On this first discovery meeting, building a vision on who you are and how your project or service can benefit your prospect should be fairly high level. You want to gauge enough interest from your prospect without overloading them. The same thing goes with a first date. Listing all the reasons why you are the perfect romantic partner and the many ways you will prove it to them will result in your date getting up and leaving. The objective is to give them enough information for them to confidently feel like they know who you are and what your project or service can bring to the table.

Master Your Elevator Pitch

You have heard the term many times before. But what exactly does it mean? And do you need to be in an elevator to use it? An elevator pitch is a short persuasive speech about yourself, your company, and your idea, project, or service. A bullet-proof elevator pitch is quick while also captivating. The name, of course, derives from the idea that you should be able to deliver your pitch within thirty to ninety seconds, the length of time on a typical elevator ride.

As an independent filmmaker, you want to be able to clearly communicate your role as a filmmaker and some background on the project you are working on or the service you are offering. If you are an experienced independent feature-film producer, you would tell your prospect you have over ten years of experience producing high-quality feature films, which includes the project you are currently working on. You would proceed to give a brief overview of what your film project is about. If you are a freelance cinematographer, you would tell your prospect you are a skilled and passionate cinematographer who has worked on a variety of projects, naming a few. Lastly, you would provide your prospect with insight on the types of services you offer.

Create and Connect Your Value Propositions

A value proposition is a valuable tool to pique your prospect's interest by communicating who you are, what your project or services consist of, and ultimately enticing this person to work with you. As a succinct explanation of both the emotional and functional benefits of your project or service, a value proposition isn't about who you are and what your project or service consists of. It touches on how it can solve your prospect's problems and complement their goals. In simple terms, your value proposition is what makes your offering unique.

You should always be trying to find ways to connect your project or service offerings to your prospect's background, goals, and pain points. Ideally, a discovery call will either establish a sales opportunity based on both parties sharing similar initiatives or it will disqualify your prospect. If you have an opportunity that aligns with the other person's wants and needs, it will be easier to get their buy-in. By establishing your project or service's value propositions before learning more about your prospect, you will effortlessly be able to strategize the flow of your discovery meeting.

Here are a few tips when establishing your value proposition:

- **Recognize the Advantages of Your Project or Service:** Make a list of all the benefits your project or service has to offer. Did your screenplay win any screenwriting competitions? Do you have a well-known actor attached to play a supporting role? Go through every area of your project, from the phenomenal characters, beautiful shooting locations, extensive post-production budget, and make note of what your prospect will most likely appreciate. You can do the same thing for the services you provide. Do you own the most cutting-edge editing software? Are you quick and reliable dealing with on-set lighting equipment? Ask yourself what you can bring to the table.

- **Describe What Makes These Advantages Valuable:** Now you have compiled a list of every benefit of your project or service, you should elaborate on why each one is potentially valuable to your prospect. For example, if you have a well-known cinema-tographer attached who is working with a state-of-the-art cam-era, this can be very valuable for the production quality of the film. If you are speaking to a distributor, this will be valuable to them because it will make it easier for them to secure exhibition channels. In addition, if you are speaking to an actress, high pro-duction quality means great captured footage of her, which in turn will enhance her performance and ultimately land her more gigs in the future. Think about how someone like your prospect would find your project or service valuable.

- **Identify Your Prospect's Main Stumbling Block:** This is per-formed after asking the right questions in your discovery call. However, through your initial research on your prospect you can collect enough information to build a few assumptions about the prospect's main problems. For example, if you are a producer and notice a screenwriter has a few scripts avail-able for option, but none of them have been produced, you can make a strong guess it's a major initiative for them to get their script made. The same thing applies if you are a set decorator. If you find out on a discovery call with a producer that their director is having a hard time finding the right kind of aesthetic for one of the locations, this information can correlate with the type of value you can provide. Keep in mind, most of this will be speculation due to not getting the full picture from the pros-pect yet. Once you hop on a discovery call with your prospect and ask them questions to gauge what their roadblocks are, you are able to effectively connect how your project or service can solve their problem.

- **Connect Your Value Proposition to Your Prospect's Problem:** Once you confidently know the prospect's roadblocks, you can proceed to connect the dots on how your project or service will help your prospect solve their problems. For example, if you are making a feature film and you are speaking to the owner of a struggling restaurant where you want to shoot a few scenes, you can connect how your film can help publicize his eatery to a whole new group of individuals. If you are talking to an investor who has disclosed he's been burned in the past by another filmmaker, you can explain how you value transparency and communication, which is highlighted in your film's business plan and other marketing materials.

- **Set Yourself Apart From Other Providers:** With so many other filmmakers out there in the world, what sets you apart from everyone else? What makes your project stand out from the rest? Whether you are a gaffer who's looking to land her next on-set gig or a producer who's trying to get funding for his film, you must be able to articulate how you are different. Your prospect has shared their goals and pain points, and it's pivotal to vocalize how your project or service is different from all the others out there providing solutions to your prospect's roadblocks.

Step #3: Schedule Next Steps

Your discovery call should be going extremely well at this point. You know this if you have successfully set an agenda and a list of questions through preliminary call planning, unearthed and intensified your prospect's pain points and goals through active listening, and built a vision on how you can help them by delivering your elevator pitch and connecting your value propositions.

More important, you have built enough rapport with your prospect and demonstrated you genuinely care about them and didn't attempt the hard sell. This is the complete opposite of what some call a "pushy car salesman." The final step in the discovery process is scheduling next steps, which happens to be the third stage in the sales process: demonstrating value.

Successful salespeople can either move into the demonstration of value phase in the same meeting or they can choose to schedule another time. Strategically, setting the meeting for another time will build a prospect's enthusiasm to learn more on how you can work together. Although you already built a vision through your elevator pitch and high-level value propositions, the demonstration of value stage is more in-depth. This is where producers will bring out their business plans and pitch decks.

At the end of your discovery call, be sure to use the statement "Based on what you have mentioned earlier, I believe our next steps should be...." If you are a producer speaking to a screenwriter about potentially optioning their screenplay, your proposed next step might be you reviewing the many ways you will be able to achieve their goals if they gave the screenplay option to you and not any other producer. If you are a filmmaker trying to secure some financing for your next project through your family friend, your next step may be to send over a detailed business plan and the shooting script. In the filmmaker's follow-up email to the potential investor, he or she can even reiterate how some of the investor's goals align with those of the filmmaker or the movie.

Discovery Summary

As the second stage of the sales process, the process of discovery is what is going to set you apart from everyone else. Especially those like you, who are aiming to get your prospect's attention. The proven and most successful way to establish a relationship with someone is through building rapport and genuinely showing interest in their hopes, fears, and dreams.

Next time you are with a salesperson and he or she is trying to hard sell you before asking you questions, you can now be certain they skipped a crucial part of the sales journey. How are they going to know what is good for you if they didn't even bother to get a glimpse of what's important to you? How are they going to know their product or service is a solution to your needs and wants? They didn't take the necessary step to find out.

Through pre-call research measures like brainstorming the right questions and building an agenda, you are demonstrating you care. As you lead your discovery meeting you are keeping it casual while simultaneously unearthing and intensifying their pain points and goals, building a vision of how you and your project or service can help them, all while actively listening to them. At the end of the discovery phase, you are directing them on the necessary next steps, which ultimately display how you and your offering can be of value to them.

In the independent filmmaking world, whether you are presenting your film to a room full of investors or demonstrating to a distributor why your film should be on their roster, the discovery stage will make your life a whole lot easier to build the relationship and ultimately get the contract signed.

CHAPTER 4
DISCOVERY—A CASE STUDY

Discovery With A Distributor

Have you ever sat down and thought about how many filmmakers there are in the world? On top of that, have you ever pondered how many films get produced every year? It's almost impossible to pin down an exact number. To give you a rough estimate, Sundance receives submissions of roughly 3,700 to 4,000 domestic films each year. With so many films being created, there aren't nearly as many distribution companies a filmmaker can work with. Do you know how many distributors there are in the United States? There are only about 55 to 60 North American distributors, which are making between 250 and 450 movies a year in total.

You can break these distributors down into four different categories:

- **The Majors** (e.g., Warner Brothers, Fox, and Paramount)

- **The Mini Majors** (e.g., Lionsgate, Miramax, Artisan)

- **The Independents** (e.g., Samuel Goldwyn, A24, and The Orchard)

- **Exploitation** (e.g., Troma, High Octane, and Concorde)

Besides producing films, distribution companies across the globe are also on the lookout for independent films to acquire. Banking on a project before it has been produced is a huge gamble for distribution companies, which is why the typically do not invest money in an unfinished product. This means the distribution company is in the business of acquiring finished films in the hopes they can market it, distribute it to their network of exhibitors, and ultimately make a good ol' profit.

Think of box-office sensations like *The Blair Witch Project*, *My Big Fat Greek Wedding*, and *Paranormal Activity*. They were all produced by independent filmmakers like you who ultimately found a distributor who shared their films with the world. Distributors are always looking for the next big hit that will cost them the least amount of money. Independent filmmakers are their favorite group because (1) there are no financial risks because the film is already finished and was paid for by your investors, and (2) you are a nobody in this town at this point and are most likely desperate and penniless after finishing your project.

If you have a completed feature film, meaning you are done with post-production, and you have already determined your distribution strategy, you are ready to submit to film festivals and reach out to distributors. If it makes sense to self-distribute your project, that is also an option to keep in mind. Since filmmakers have more direct access to their audience than ever before, traditional distribution companies are in decline. The arrival of the internet and social media platforms have completely changed the game, resulting in a filmmaker's ability to directly connect with consumers and cut the middleman out.

Hopefully you should have done your research on the best distribution strategy for your film way back in development and pre-production. A filmmaker must ask: *What is the best strategy for the type of project I am creating?* For example, a heavy drama character piece with a well-known actress would have a good chance of premiering at a major Tier 1 film festival like Sundance, Tribeca, or Cannes. Distributors can try to compete for your film, giving you more leverage for a better distribution deal. On the other hand, if your project is a low-budget one-location horror film with a non-recognizable cast, signing on a distributor and going straight to Video on Demand would be your best bet. This is because the likelihood your film would get accepted into a festival and ultimately hold up against the other titles with more recognizable talent and higher budgets is very slim. You should always aim to submit your film into a Tier 1 festival first because it will give you more leverage with distributors. When submitting to a distributor, keep in mind that your film must be in a polished state, meaning it's in the best possible shape, before you share a screener of your movie.

This case study on the discovery stage is centered on a hypothetical discovery meeting a filmmaker would have with a prospective acquisitions executive at a distribution company after sending their initial outreach email with the call-to-action of watching a screener of their film. At this point, the filmmaker has reached out to twenty distribution companies and has received five offers. The goal of the discovery call is to vet the distributor to ensure they would be the best possible partner for their film.

Phase 1—Planning the Distribution Discovery

Before you can confidently hop on a call with a distributor to find out if they are the best choice for your film, you must do some pre-discovery call planning. In the prospecting phase you should have already gathered enough information on the background of the distribution company and some of the titles they have worked on by looking at their website and IMDb profile. Since they responded to your outreach, watched your screener, and want to strike a deal with you, it's now time to plan your discovery call to ensure you have all the facts in front of you.

Step #1: Use Online Resources to Create Questions to Ask the Distributor

As you have learned in the prospecting stage, the internet is your best friend when it comes to uncovering all you need to know about a person or a company. Most importantly, it will assist you in asking the right questions and establishing your discovery call agenda. You should not only do research on the distribution company but also on the acquisition executive you are speaking to, using the same methods found in the prospecting stage.

Here is a list of online resources you can use when planning for your discovery call with a distributor:

- **IMDbPro:** One of the most popular entertainment industry online databases, IMDb provides users with cast and production crew contact information, personal biographies, project information, plot summaries, ratings, and more. Originated in 1990, IMDb's database has grown to approximately 6.5 million titles and 10.4 million people, as well as 83 million registered users. Although it costs money to sign up for an account, IMDbPro is a necessary tool in the research phase of securing distribution for your project. Going to a distributor's IMDb page, you can see an entire list of every film they have distributed and what rights they have. For example, you can see if they have all media or only theatrical rights, along with worldwide versus only domestic rights. Potential questions you can ask can be centered on how they plan to distribute your film and whether it would be only Video on Demand or if it would include theatrical, DVD, or broadcast. On some of the projects you can even see the budget amount and gross earnings. IMDb also lists the names and job titles of the company's personnel so you can easily identify the best person to contact. Lastly, looking at the list of films the distribution company has worked with in the past, you can see the production companies of each film and the appropriate contact. You should reach out to this person to get honest feedback on their experience working with the distributor.

- **Their Website:** The distributor's website should tell a convincing story about their experience and success in the business of distributing films. Read about the company, the executives, and some of the relationships they have with exhibition channels. Read all the press kits, case studies, testimonials, and any other information providing insight on their process and overall success. You don't want to rely only on their word, especially when it comes to testimonials. Of course a distributor will share only positive feedback and refer you to talk to only happy clients. You want to do the research yourself by getting in touch with a filmmaker they have worked with in the past on one of their random titles. Taking some of the sales collateral on their website, you can develop some specific questions referring to their strategy in distributing one of their films and how they achieved success.

- **Exhibition Channels:** Taking the list of films from their website or IMDb profile, do a Google search of where you can rent or purchase these titles. Are they available only on Transactional Video on Demand (TVOD) websites like Amazon? Are they also available on Subscription Video on Demand (SVOD) options like Netflix and Hulu? Can you purchase a DVD on Walmart or Best Buy? Are any of their films available on cable or broadcast television channels? It's a red flag if you are having trouble finding a way to get access to the movie. There can be a lot of reasons for this, including the distributor having a lack of relationships with online and offline exhibition platforms. Formulate questions centered on what exhibition channels they have relationships with and their intended distribution strategy for your film.

- **Online and Offline Film Publicity and Marketing:** Taking your investigation on the distributor's film titles one step further, you should do an internet search on any sort of news article, interview, or press coverage on any of the movies they distributed, including their most recent titles. Part of a distributor's main responsibilities is to market your film to the masses with the goal of turning these audiences into paying customers. If you barely notice any sort of marketing and publicity campaigns on their titles, it's a major red flag. Coming up with questions on their marketing and publicity tactics and how they would potentially promote your film is something you should inquire about.

Step #2: Create A List of Questions Based on Your Research

Now that you have finished researching the distribution company, the titles they have distributed, along with a background on the acquisitions executive, you are ready to create a list of questions to ask during your discovery meeting.

In Figure 4A you can see a list of questions a filmmaker would construct after thoroughly researching a distribution company and executive before a discovery meeting.

FIGURE 4A   DISCOVERY QUESTION EXAMPLES

- What did you like about my film?
- I saw that your most recent title, NAME OF MOVIE, was in TVOD for only a few months before it was placed on Netflix and Hulu. How long do you typically keep your titles in each digital streaming stage?
- That's awesome you have been with the company for over 10 years now. What are you most proud of at your time with the company?
- What do you find most valuable about my film?
- What are the distribution company goals this year in regard to the acquisition of new titles?
- What do you find to be the company's major roadblocks?
- What distribution methods do you see yourself using to find the right audience?
- Looking at your film, MOVIE TITLE, I noticed that you guys went straight to Video on Demand on select platforms. Given that my film is similar in genre, budget, and cast level, would you take the same approach?
- What did you have in mind for the rollout strategy specifically for my title?
- I discovered that for a majority of the films you have distributed in the past, you were only handling the US theatrical rights and not all media, including digital. Can you explain why that is?
- I didn't see very many interviews or news articles centered on the release of both MOVIE TITLE and MOVIE TITLE. What types of marketing do you do to inform the general public about the release of one of your titles?
- I see that a lot of your titles have gotten press from *IndieWire* and *Hollywood Reporter.* Tell me about your relationship with each one.
- What types of films would you say your company is passionate about? Do they all share a common theme?

Continued

- I recently spoke to a filmmaker, NAME, about one of your films, MOVIE TITLE. He told me that he wished there had been more marketing tactics employed when the film was released. How are you going to market and publicize my film?
- It says on your website that you guys describe your films as "tribal" and that you are looking for films that have pre-existing audiences. Do you believe there is a pre-existing audience for my film? If so, who are these people and how do you find them?
- What do you see as a viable return for a film like mine?

The filmmaker jotted down every question on their mind when embarking on their research expedition. Now that they have a variety of potential questions to ask during the discovery meeting, the next step is to organize the questions in a way that breaks them into specific categories. In Figure 4B you can see the filmmaker decided to break the questions into four categories: general, rollout strategy, marketing and publicity strategy, and, lastly, company and acquisition executive–focused questions.

FIGURE 4B   CATEGORIZED DISCOVERY QUESTIONS - EXAMPLE

General Questions on My Film:
- What did you like about my film?
- What do you find most valuable about my film compared to other titles?
- What do you see as a viable return for a film like mine?

Rollout Strategy Questions:
- I saw that your most recent title, NAME OF MOVIE, was in TVOD for only a few months before it was placed on Netflix and Hulu. How long do you typically keep your titles in each digital streaming stage?
- What distribution methods do you see yourself using to find the right audience?
- Looking at your film MOVIE TITLE, I noticed that you guys went straight to Video on Demand on select platforms. Given that my film is similar in genre, budget, and cast level, would you take the same approach?
- What did you have in mind for the rollout strategy specifically for my title?

Continued

- I discovered that a for majority of the films you have distributed in the past, you were only handling the US theatrical rights and not all media, including digital. Can you explain why that is?

Marketing and Publicity Strategy Questions:
- I didn't see very many interviews and news articles centered on the release of MOVIE TITLE and MOVIE TITLE. What type of marketing do you do to inform the general public about the release of one of your titles?
- I see that a lot of your titles have gotten press from *IndieWire* and *Hollywood Reporter*. Tell me about your relationship with each.
- I recently spoke to a filmmaker, NAME, of one of your films, MOVIE TITLE. He told me that he wished there had been more marketing tactics employed when the film was released. How are you going to market and publicize my film?

Company and Acquisition Executive Specific Questions:
- That's awesome you have been with the company for over 10 years now. What are you most proud of at your time with the company?
- What are the distribution company goals this year in regard to the acquisition of new titles?
- What do you find to be the company's major roadblocks?
- What types of films would you say your company is passionate about? Do they all share a common theme?
- It says on your website that you guys describe your films as "tribal" and that you are looking for films that have pre-existing audiences. Do you believe there is a pre-existing audience for my film? If so, who are these people and how do you find them?

Arranging the questions in this format will not only help you stay organized, it will also help you identify the potential areas you should discuss with the distributor on your discovery call. How does one go about outlining the topics of discussion for a discovery call? Simply create a call agenda.

Step #3: Create A Call Agenda Based on Your List of Questions

In the last stage of planning your discovery call, you are going to want to take the questions you have created from your research and build a call agenda to ensure the conversation stays on track. On top of putting your agenda in your email's calendar invitation, you want to draft a short script highlighting your points of discussion. This agenda will be delivered after the initial three-to ten-minute rapport-building stage of the call.

FIGURE 4C   MEETING AGENDA SCRIPT

"Thanks again for hopping on a call! Before we dive into everything, I want to make sure we are on the same page to ensure we're being respectful of each other's time. With that being said, I'd like to ask general questions surrounding my film, along with rollout, marketing and publicity strategies, and questions centered on the company. Does that sound good to you?"

Notice how in Figure 4C the independent filmmaker thanked the distributor for their time and proceeded to change gears to talk business? The filmmaker proceeds to briefly list the areas they want to cover on the call. Expressing how you are mindful of your prospect's time and confirming that your agenda is aligned with their intentions of the call is a courtesy that will convey to them you are respectful and professional.

Now that you have your discovery questions put together and your call agenda script written, you are ready to proceed to the next stage of discovery: leading the meeting.

Phase 2—Leading the Distribution Discovery Call

The filmmaker is now either standing next to or is on the phone with the distributor, and it's time for the filmmaker to lead the discovery call. The meeting should only take about thirty minutes and the filmmaker must strategically use those thirty minutes to obtain the goal of vetting this potential distributor. There are only a few major areas of leading the discovery call, including building rapport, unearthing and intensifying pain points, and building a vision. Here is how the filmmaker performs all of them during a thirty-minute conversation.

The First Six Minutes—Build Rapport

Step #1: Ask General Opening Questions

Instead of jumping right into business, the filmmaker leading the discovery call decides to start off very casual and fun. Since the whole point of building rapport is finding common ground and ultimately establishing trust and confidence with your prospect, asking fun and entertaining questions will do exactly that.

In Figure 4D you will find a list of some general questions the filmmaker has asked the distributor within the first five minutes of the conversation.

FIGURE 4D   RAPPORT BUILDING QUESTIONS

- How's this (day of the week) treating you?
- I see you guys are based out of _____. I actually was out there a few months ago and visited my friend. What area of the city do you live in?
- Are you planning on going to Cannes next month for the festival? Have you been before?
- While I was preparing for this call, I noticed that you were connected with _____ on LinkedIn. I actually know _____ too. How did you meet?
- Are you watching anything good on Netflix right now?

The filmmaker used creative questions based on the research they did, while at the same time not coming off like they creepily followed them on the internet. Asking the distributor about shared connections, the location where they work, future career plans, and their favorite television shows are all acceptable topics the filmmaker can chat about in the rapport-building stage of the conversation.

Step #2: Dive into Call Agenda

When the filmmaker notices a moment of silence or senses a rushed energy from the distributor, it's time to talk business by diving into the call agenda. Using the script found in Figure 4C, the filmmaker sets the stage for what the conversation will entail.

When delivering your call agenda, be sure you are not sounding robotic and especially not like you are reading from a script. Keep it as natural and friendly as possible and be sure to pay attention to your tone of voice. A sense of enthusiasm should be detected in your voice as you go over the topics you want to cover during your call.

7 to 20 Minutes—Unearth and Intensify Goals and Pain Points

Now that the filmmaker has delivered their call agenda, they can now jump into each category's list of questions. Taking the questions they put together in Figure 4B, the filmmaker is also being sure to further investigate some of the distributor's answers. For example, when the distributor answers the question regarding the company's major roadblocks, the filmmaker proceeds to collect even further information. Some of the distributor's potential roadblocks can include negative feedback from past filmmakers, a lack of exhibitor relationships, a lack of talent and resources working at the company, and more. Of course the acquisition executive will never want to provide you with too much information on the company's pain points, because he or she is ultimately trying to sell you on signing a distribution deal with them. However, don't be afraid to challenge the executive to find out more. Knowing some of their pain points will help you in not only vetting the best possible distributor but also increase your leverage when it comes time to making a deal.

Understanding the different types of pain points and goals, the filmmaker takes the distributor's answers and quickly jots down a few notes on a notepad.

FIGURE 4E   PAIN POINTS AND GOAL BREAKDOWN

Pain Points:

Support - They don't have as much leverage with major streaming partners like Netflix and Hulu, nor do most of their films make it to DVD to be sold in big box retailers like Target and Walmart.

Support - It seems to be a very small team at the company, which possibly will make it hard to get things done for my film.

Process - They don't have any insight on sales conversion rates for VOD, only VOD projections.

Process - One of the filmmakers I spoke to said that quarterly payments are usually delayed, and it turns out the company installed a new accounting system, which they are still getting used to.

Goals:

Outcome Goal - They want to be known exclusively for psychological thrillers. My film is a psychological thriller.

Process Goal - They want to develop strong relationships with their filmmakers and provide ultimate transparency and support. They want to partner with filmmakers who continually produce films.

Performance Goal - They want to expand their international sales representation endeavors and not only focus on domestic distribution. I'm in search of an international sales agent as well, so this may be a good fit.

Through their questions, the filmmaker has unearthed valuable information that will contribute to the goal of vetting the distributor to see if they would be a good choice. For example, acknowledging the distribution company's goal of being known for psychological thrillers, their pain point of delayed payments to filmmakers due to a new accounting system and their lack of personnel, the filmmaker can use this information for leverage. Of course, the acquisitions executive wants to make a deal with the filmmaker, but now the filmmaker has the ability to go after the best possible deal now that they are aware of the distributor's roadblocks and objectives.

20 to 25 Minutes—Build a Vision

This is the point in the call when the filmmaker takes all the information received from the distributor's answers to the questions and frames themself and their project as the ultimate solution. Although the filmmaker most likely provided a brief introduction on who they are and how their project developed, this is the point in the conversation where they dive into who they are.

Step #3: Deliver Your Elevator Pitch

Because the distributor most likely did some research on the filmmaker before hopping on a call, the filmmaker doesn't need to get too granule in sharing their background. The filmmaker should also provide a high-level introduction in the beginning of the discovery meeting to provide the distributor with some context. In Figure 4F you can see how the filmmaker provides the distributor with enough information to get them excited.

FIGURE 4F   FILMMAKER ELEVATOR PITCH - EXAMPLE

"As I've stated earlier in our call, I've been an independent filmmaker for over six years now and have had three projects distributed with other companies. Having had not such great experiences with them, I'm looking for a distributor who is super passionate about my film and who is looking to build a long-term relationship, since I'm always working on new projects. Given that my film has a high production quality and a supporting cast of familiar talent, I think it can potentially be a good fit for you. Based on everything we've talked about, I feel like we may share similar goals."

Step #4: Connect Your Value Propositions

After the filmmaker delivers their elevator pitch, it's time for them to go one step further and specifically repeat back some of the distributors pain points and goals. They ultimately want to outline how they fit into the filmmaker's value propositions.

FIGURE 4G   FILMMAKER VALUE PROPOSITIONS - EXAMPLE

"To make sure we're on the same page, it looks like your goals are to build a portfolio of groundbreaking psychological thrillers, establish long-term relationships with your filmmakers, and even start representing more films for international sales?

"That's awesome to hear because I'm personally super passionate about psychological thrillers, and I've got a ton of ideas and projects in the works. I'm also in need of international sales representation and can possibly use you for that as well. Luckily, we started marketing the project early on in pre-production and already have a fan-base of 10,000 followers on Instagram.

"Given what you said about your team being fairly small, your limited relationships with the major streaming platforms, and limited insight on VOD sales conversion rates, what would you guys be willing to offer me that I can't get from another distributor? As you can see, my film is very high quality with a B-level actor attached, so it should be fairly easy to exhibit."

In Figure 4G the filmmaker summarizes the distributor's goals and roadblocks, all while simultaneously providing the value of their project. By doing this it's clearly cementing the idea the acquisition executive would be a fool to not offer you a healthy deal. Toward the end of their statement, the filmmaker also challenges them on how they would be different from any other distribution company in terms of strategy. This is a technique that can demonstrate one's leverage, especially if there is a bidding war with other distributors. If you have five discovery calls like this with other distributors, you can easily pit their deals against each other and formulate the best possible deal for yourself.

Phase 3—Scheduling the Distributor Discovery Call
Next Steps

The Last Five Minutes—Next Steps

The last five minutes of the thirty-minute conversation, the filmmaker is focused on next steps. After talking to the acquisition executive and getting the opportunity to ask detailed questions about the company and their strategies, the filmmaker can make a good estimate on whether the distribution company would be a good fit for them. If so, the filmmaker would possibly suggest next steps consisting of the distributor drafting up a domestic distribution deal, or a follow-up call to discuss international sales strategy in further detail. Using the phrase "based on what you mentioned earlier, I believe our next steps should be…" the filmmaker decides it would make sense to gather some more feedback from other filmmakers the distribution company has worked with in the past before they sign a deal with them.

Case Study—A Final Word on Discovery

Identifying the right distributor for your project will either make or break your project's ultimate success. By doing the necessary pre-discovery plan of researching the distributor, brainstorming questions, and creating a call agenda, you are ensuring a productive conversation around topics that contribute to your goal of vetting the distributor. Leading your discovery by establishing rapport, uncovering and intensifying goals and roadblocks, and building a vision around your project will guarantee your ability to negotiate a deal that serves your best interests. Lastly, establishing the necessary steps to move the relationship to the next stage will set the seal for both parties.

When negotiating with a distributor, it's recommended to not provide any sort of sneak previews. You want to ensure they are seeing the most professional version; this will mitigate the risk of you and your project looking amateurish. If given the opportunity, you should also screen the film to a crowd consisting of multiple distributors. This is because it will cause a frenzy and result in the distributors competing against each other, which puts you in a more powerful position. Lastly, you want to sell your film when buyers are prospecting for product. Major film markets, such as the American Film Market in Santa Monica, Cannes in France, and the European Film Market in Berlin, are places where distributors acquire and sell titles.

When it comes to discovery, the main takeaway, whether you are dealing with a distribution company, a financier, an actress, or a location manager, is that you must be sure to establish the relationship on the right foot. Even if you technically should be considered the prospect on the call, with a distributor trying to persuade you to sign with them, you should always take the time to do your due diligence and get to know the other person. By asking thoughtful questions and figuring out some of their goals and roadblocks, you are separating yourself from all the other filmmakers they are having conversations with. Being known as the person who took the time to learn about someone and who is genuinely interested in developing a partnership that works for both parties will serve you well in the entertainment industry.

STAGE III

DEMONSTRATING VALUE

CHAPTER 5
DEMONSTRATE VALUE

Defining Value Demonstration

The third step in the sales process is where the salesperson takes everything they have learned from their prospect in the previous discovery stage and shows how their product or service will ultimately benefit them. Whether it's through sharing personal success stories or employing statistics and hard data, value demonstration is all about fully convincing your prospect on what you are offering.

Value-based selling is a strategy consisting of a consultative approach, leading to educating and helping a prospect in seeing the potential value the product or service can provide. Educating your prospect on a topic will position you as a resource of information, which will assist in establishing trust, confidence, and overall credibility. A prospect is more likely to strike a deal with the person who brings something valuable to the table. It's how you demonstrate that value that makes a world of difference.

Value Demonstration Goals

Demonstrating value is a key stage in the sales process to make certain you are:

- Putting the needs and goals of your prospect first

- Using methods to articulate the value of your product or service

- Establishing yourself as a source of expertise on your industry, project, or service

Value Demonstration Steps

There are three key steps in the undertaking of value demonstration: developing enough knowledge of your product or service, using storytelling to convey favorable outcomes, and building sales materials that reinforce value.

Step #1: Develop Knowledge of Your Product or Service

Before you can fully articulate the value of your product or service, you must be fully trained on every aspect. Not only do you need to have knowledge of every area of your offering, but you must also have a general idea of the industry you work in, along with the industry your prospect is a part of.

Developing knowledge of your product or service consists of investing the time to perform regular training habits, and putting your knowledge into action through a variety of methods, ensuring you are putting yourself in your prospect's shoes. These two areas are requisite steps in effectively expressing your expertise to others and building a sense of trust and credibility.

In independent filmmaking, one must develop knowledge of their industry, their film project, and their specialties to convince others on their ability to get the job done. Whether it's a producer persuading a film investor to contribute half a million dollars toward their feature film, or a cinematographer convincing a director of their knowledge and expertise of light, filters, and lenses, both individuals need to fully train on every possible characteristic it takes to succeed in convincing the other person.

Invest the Time

This won't be the last time you hear the words "practice makes perfect." However, if you hope to become an expert in something, you must clock in a great deal of hours. According to author Malcom Gladwell in his book *Outliers*, to be considered an expert in something takes at least ten thousand hours of practice. It's not imperative for you to have ten thousand hours in order to be able to articulate product knowledge. However, this should give you an idea of the type of time you need to invest to fully grasp the ins and outs of something.

There are a variety of ways one can learn about their industry, product, or service, including:

- **Hands-on Experience:** The most basic way one can learn about a specific topic is to go out into the world and perform some sort of action. Whether it's volunteering, working, or completing an internship, there are many ways one can acquire hands-on experience. Hands-on experiences use both kinesthetic and tactile methods, where smell, sight, touch, feel, taste, and hearing can enrich your mind and ultimately help you retain what you learn for a longer period of time. Working on multiple short films, volunteering at a film festival, or landing an assistant editing position at a post-production facility are all examples of how an independent filmmaker can use hands-on experience to further their knowledge. By networking with other independent filmmakers in your area and searching the internet for job and internship opportunities in the entertainment industry, you will be getting one step closer to becoming an expert in your field. I recommend using social media sites like Facebook and Reddit to find a community of filmmakers based near you. Offer to work on a few projects for free to build up your resume. You can also find local filmmaking jobs on websites like Entertainment-Career.net and Productionhub.com.

- **Education:** With so many developments in modern technology and the amount of resources available at our fingertips, there is no reason for you to have to get a bachelor's degree in film at

UCLA or NYU in order to be successful. Of course, having a college degree will contribute to your ability to establish trustworthiness, but it's by no means a prerequisite to becoming a filmmaker. Nowadays, there are so many available educational options for you to fully immerse yourself in a particular topic. Whether it's taking a class on screenwriting at your local community college, a four-hour online course on cinematography, or a two-day film producing conference, the opportunities are endless. I highly recommend taking Dov S-S Simens' 2-Day Film School course, as it does a phenomenal job of highlighting every facet of independent filmmaking in a clear and concise way. Some additional online education websites I recommend include Udemy.com, Coursera.com, and Futurelearn.com. Type in whatever topic you want to educate yourself on, and they will most likely have multiple class offerings available.

- **Books:** There are thousands of digital and hard copy books available on the topic of independent filmmaking. Whether you are trying to understand the industry as a whole or your specific line of work within the industry, reading a book will expand your mindset in a multitude of ways. I recommend reading the book *Down and Dirty Pictures: Miramax, Sundance, and the Rise of Independent Film* by Peter Biskind to get better acquainted with the independent film industry. If you are a producer, I recommend reading specific manuals on producing like *Indie Film Producing: The Craft of Low Budget Filmmaking* by Suzanne Lyons. The same advice goes if you are a director or cinematographer. Read books about your specific craft and enlighten yourself on areas you may not have known about. The same holds true for books about your film project. I recommend reading *The Declaration of Independent Filmmaking* by Jonathan Sheldon. If you have recently produced a feature film, it would be advantageous to read books about how to successfully deal with the post-production process, marketing your movie on social media, obtaining domestic distribution and international sales representation, and more.

- **Online Media:** There are endless possibilities when it comes to finding an answer to your questions nowadays. By asking Siri or Google a question, you are immediately directed to the appropriate resource. Online media include everything from YouTube videos on how to put together a shooting schedule, online courses on how to direct actors, a blog post on the complexities of film production tax incentives, and more. Whatever topic you want to learn more about is at your fingertips. Podcasts are another form of online media you can use to gather knowledge on broad and specific topics. For example, as a filmmaker you can tune in to either podcasts consisting of a general exploration of filmmaking or something very specific like film editing. One podcast I highly recommend is Alex Ferrari's *Indie Film Hustle,* which examines every facet of the independent filmmaking process through interviews with a variety of professionals.

- **Informational Interviews:** An informational interview is a meeting in which one person approaches another with the clear goal of obtaining career and work-related knowledge and advice from the other person. The goal of the meeting is not to land a job like in a traditional interview. If you want to learn more about a certain topic as an independent filmmaker, one approach would be to reach out to a professional in the topic you are attempting to learn more about. Sitting down with this person and asking them questions about their experience and background will help paint a full picture of the information you are seeking. For instance, a filmmaker who wants to learn more about the process of international sales can reach out to an international sales agent with the clear agenda of asking them questions to gain a better understanding of the international sales process. A screenwriter can reach out to another more established writer to ask questions about techniques in creating characters and outlining plot points. I recommend using tools like IMDbPro and LinkedIn to locate the appropriate people and contacting them via email to schedule a casual conversation over coffee or over the phone.

- **News:** It's without question that a person should be aware about what's going on in the world that indirectly and directly can affect them and their business endeavors. Stock market investors are always paying attention to financial news to ensure their stocks are doing well. As an independent filmmaker, it's important to know any sort of relevant changes, advancements, and critical updates within the industry. Not only will reading the news contribute to you establishing credibility, it will also arm you with topics to chat about in rapport-building scenarios. Some of the major news outlets you should pay attention to as an independent filmmaker include *IndieWire, Filmmaker Magazine, Deadline, Hollywood Reporter,* and *Variety.*

Put Knowledge into Action

Now that you have obtained the knowledge of your industry, product, or service, it's time to take it one step further by putting your knowledge into action. The only way to internalize your understanding of a certain subject is to practice your knowledge with some form of action.

Here are few ways you can effectively put obtained knowledge into action:

- **Tell Someone Else What You Have Learned:** When you spread the word about the knowledge you have obtained, you are hitting two birds with one stone. This is because that while introducing others to a new topic, you are also reminding yourself what you have learned. Every single time you repeat a piece of mastery, you are deep-rooting the idea more and more into your mind. You also will have an easier time remembering a piece of information if you tell it to others. Continually remembering the knowledge you obtained will result in you putting those ideas into action. If a filmmaker learns about the components needed to result in a picture lock before moving on to audio mixing and shares it with another filmmaker, the act of them talking about it and repeating what they learned will aid the filmmaker in successfully following the protocol needed.

■ **Take Notes:** As you consume new information, it's helpful to write everything down on a piece of paper or type it into your phone. By making a list of the things you've learned, you can also make a list of the things you personally need to do. For example, if a producer has learned about the process it takes to establish a limited liability corporation for their production company, the producer can jot down a list of steps they need to take to successfully achieve this for their own company. Putting your thoughts into writing will make it more concrete and ultimately will hold you accountable in making sure you follow through with it.

■ **Include Ideas into Your Routine:** If you want to fully embrace and internalize the knowledge you have obtained in an action-oriented way, discover a way you can include it in your daily or weekly routine. For instance, if a filmmaker wants to understand budgeting techniques for feature films, they can make it a goal to calculate the budget for each of the film's critical departments, including below-the-line and above-the-line costs. The filmmaker can even take it one step further and practice budgeting measures on a personal level by calculating their personal financial expenditures. If you are struggling with committing to incorporating your knowledge into your routine, you can request the help of an accountability partner or set daily calendar reminders to yourself.

■ **Role-Play:** Role-playing consists of a scenario and set of roles with the goal of fully internalizing knowledge and putting it into practice. By first identifying the situation and adding details about the particular topic, you and a friend can create a scenario resulting in a role-playing activity. When assigning roles, whether you want to play the prospect and your friend plays the expert, it's critical you put yourself in the minds of the people you are representing. This involves understanding their perspectives, goals, motivations, and feelings in regard to the situation and topic. It's time to act it out as if you are running through a scenario with the real stakeholders. When the role-play is finished, it's important to discuss with your partner the many things you learned in the activity so you can bring this obtained knowledge to the real experience. If a filmmaker is about to have a sales presentation to investors pitching a new feature film, they can set up a role-play scenario and pretend to be the investor while another person can pretend to be them. In the activity, the filmmaker can get the opportunity to step into the shoes of a potential investor and ask all the potential questions an investor would want to know before handing over their money. Most importantly, by role-playing as the investor, the filmmaker can identify potential objections and fears that may result in them not signing a check.

Step #2: Use Storytelling

In order to demonstrate value to someone, you must be able to clearly articulate the value in a way that will connect with them on a human level. Storytelling is an ancient art form and overall valuable form of human expression. It's been around since the beginning of time and has served a purpose of communicating one's experiences to those around them. In fact, the true essence of storytelling can be found in the entire process of filmmaking. A screenplay and a motion picture consist of a story centered on a protagonist, and the story takes place in a particular location, during a specified a time period, and involves specific people.

Telling compelling stories takes practice, like anything else. There are three main components found in captivating tales: a dose of emotion and feeling that reaches the audience, personal narratives that communicate a unique background and experiences, and lastly, the application of accurate story structure, all of which guarantee an emotional roller-coaster ride for listeners.

Inject Emotion

It's interesting to think about how two individuals can tell the same story but obtain different results. One can catch the attention of everyone in the audience, whereas another can have everyone in the audience checking their phones. Of course, while our goal should be to always share exciting stories, it's important to realize that it's not the content making the difference; it's how we express our emotions. Every story has what is called an emotional core, which conveys how the storyteller feels about the events they are describing. Without expressing emotions while delivering a story, it makes it harder for the audience to relate and fully comprehend the story you are sharing. Since storytelling is all about connecting with people on a human level, how do you expect to connect with someone if they can't capture your feelings and emotions in the process?

For an independent filmmaker, injecting emotion into your personal stories will show your prospect how passionate you are about your endeavors. While a producer tries to convince an owner of a potential shooting location to let them shoot there, the producer can share how exciting it was for another location owner they have worked with in the past to shoot a real movie in their little coffee shop. The producer can also mention how extremely happy the owner was to see the amount of social media buzz the coffee shop got after the shoot. A filmmaker speaking to a potential distributor about their movie can share how the standing ovation at the recent film festival premiere made them feel. Evoking commentary on your emotions and feelings while sharing your story will make a world of difference.

Share Your Narrative

Have you ever listened to someone highlight every little detail in their story and ultimately you find yourself lost with what's going on? Extraneous information slows a story down and leaves audiences confused. How do you know the difference between what's considered extra and what's considered essential? It all starts with your personal narrative. With your personal background and experiences being so unique to you, the story starts way before the main event. You don't need to share your entire life story in order to be able to effectively communicate what happened to you last Tuesday. However, you must ask yourself why you were personally involved. Sometimes it makes sense to back up a bit and fill your listeners in on background information that may or may not have made sense in the beginning of your tale. The places where you grew up, the values you adopted during your childhood, your top five biggest fears—these are some examples contributing to your unique narrative. Mentioning how you moved to Los Angeles from Salt Lake City four years ago might be helpful in understanding why you were so scared about the earthquake two weeks ago. A story about how you made your child return an item they shoplifted might be elevated by sharing the values your parents taught you while growing up.

It makes sense for a director to talk about growing up in a poverty-stricken area of Chicago to convey how a screenplay is closely connected with their life. The same goes for a producer chatting with a British-based post-production studio. Mentioning their experience living in London for four years will provide greater context when mentioning how they have come to appreciate British cinema. If your listener might not relate to your narrative, you can always mention the narrative of someone else in the story. For example, bringing up how your cinematographer from Sweden always loves to visit Los Angeles and enjoy the sunny, 70-degree weather might be a good piece of information to share when speaking to a financier from Sweden.

Apply Story Structure

Who would have thought story structure was needed for more than screenplays and books? One must also follow a story structure when delivering personal stories. I won't dive into specific details on how to plot a story, but here are a few tips on applying good story structure:

- **Climax:** Every story has something called a climax. A climax is the huge important event and ultimately the impetus for why you are sharing the story in the first place. For instance, the climax of a story centered on how your film won an award at a film festival would be the moment you accepted the award in front of the audience.

- **Controlling Idea:** Stories consist of another element called a controlling idea. A controlling idea is the underlying reason for the changes occurring in your story and why the event happened in the first place. A director's controlling idea on how they ended up with a certain angle for one of their shots might be the way the light from outside was positioned at the time of day.

- **Moral (or Purpose) and Personal Connection:** You should aim to always have a clear moral or purpose in the stories you share, which serves to explain why you are telling your audience in the first place. It should also have some sort of personal connection, whether it's yourself or someone else you are connected to. Sharing a story about the personal experience of an actress you have worked with in the past or telling a personal story about what it was like to shoot a film on a boat in the Atlantic Ocean are two examples. The moral or purpose of telling these stories can be identified by asking yourself why you are bringing it up in the first place. Talking on the phone with an actress who shares her concern of riding a motorcycle in a scene might prompt you to disclose a similar story you heard from another actress you have worked with in the past.

- **Pacing:** Being a filmmaker, you are very aware there is a beginning, middle, and end to every story. Jumping around on the timeline will result in massive confusion by your audience. Like any conventional Hollywood family film, keep it simple and in order. If you attempted to tell your stories the way Tarantino does, using nonlinear methods, including flashbacks and flash-forwards, your audience would be looking at you with an open mouth. Don't make things complicated. Set the stage on where your story begins and the events that took place and how you reached your story's climax.

- **Details, Details, and More Details:** Never assume your audience already knows all the specifics of your story, especially when it comes to how someone or something in your story looks or acts. Providing more context will paint a better picture and ultimately make your story more interesting and enjoyable. However, you want to refrain from providing too many details, or you risk your prospect losing attention or possibly getting confused. For example, when attempting to share the differences between two actresses' auditions, the director can provide insight on how both actresses physically differed from each other, along with their contrasts in personalities.

Step #3: Build Sales Materials

Being able to effectively develop a knowledge base of your industry, project, or service, along with sharing compelling stories that inject emotion and excite listeners, are important undertakings in demonstrating value to your prospects. To further increase a salesperson's ability to exhibit their project or service's worthiness, a salesperson might also consider building a variety of visual materials called sales collateral. The focus of sales collateral is to build credibility and provide additional information to prospective buyers to help influence their purchasing decisions. Customer testimonials highlighting positive interactions, case studies of successful campaigns with similar clients, and one-sheets providing statistical research centered on the product's solution are all examples of materials salespeople use to influence a potential customer.

In the world of independent filmmaking, you may not be creating one-sheets with statistical research on how your film compares with, say, *Titanic* or a case study on how you survived working with a tough director of photography. However, there are five major types of sales materials you should be aware of and ultimately create:

- **Business Plans:** In short, a business plan is a document that sets out a business's future objectives and the strategies that will be implemented to achieve them. In the case of a filmmaker, if you expect individuals to invest their hard-earned money into your movie, it's imperative you have a proposal outlining exactly what you plan to do with the money. Business plans include major sections like company and personnel biographies, an overview of the project and the industry as a whole, risk management details, distribution and marketing strategies, and plenty more.

Everything from proposed budgets, shooting schedules, and projected investment returns are covered to satisfy questions on every aspect of the project, along with your overall potential investor's peace of mind. Expressing all the potential risks your investor might face by investing in your film is an important part of your business plan because it establishes transparency and trust. Thoroughly outlining the potential monetary and non-monetary profits your investor can gain by cutting you a check should increase your odds of success.

- **Pitch Decks:** A pitch deck is essentially a high-level presentation of your film project or suite of services. Powerful pitch decks for projects include an introduction to the story, characters, locations, and themes, along with biographical information on the key filmmakers involved. Project-based pitch decks also can include distribution and marketing strategies, musical score, and the director's vision on camera style and tone. It's one thing to have your prospect read your script. It's a whole other level if you can provide them with a vibrant document encapsulating the story in a visual way. Pitch decks centered on freelance services like post-production editing, special effects work, or cinematography should include a background on yourself, examples of your past work or relevant websites (and links that take a prospect there), along with any past client testimonials. Pitch decks should also include your contact information so that your prospect knows how to get in touch with you.

- **Demo Reels and Trailers:** Because filmmaking is a video-based art form, it makes sense for a filmmaker to have video examples of their work. Whether you are a freelance color corrector, editor, cinematographer, director, or sound designer, it's essential you have videos of your work to show prospective clients. A demo reel is a trailer of your work. There are many examples available on the internet of beautiful demo reels. It's important to include your name and contact information and to keep the demo reel fairly short in length. A few minutes are enough to be able to convey the value of your service. A filmmaker can also use a trailer of their film to elicit interest from distributors, sales agents, and online audiences to check out the full version of the movie. By deconstructing the film and not giving away too many details, a ninety-second to two-minute trailer can infuse excitement in your prospect. Even if you haven't started filming your movie yet, putting together a short teaser trailer to show investors might be enough to get them enthusiastic about the project.

- **Case Studies and Testimonials:** A case study is a research method involving an up-close and in-depth analysis of a particular case. For example, if you are a freelance editor, a case study might include information about a project in which you were hired after an initial editor worked on it, which includes how the edit of the film looked before you were hired and how it looked once you completed the project. Giving specific examples of editing methods you used to make the film look better than it did, along with quotes from your client regarding your great work, are all very helpful information to include in your case study. Testimonials are also very valuable sales collateral because they show you have done similar work for other people and those people were pleased with the results. For an independent filmmaker, having five positive testimonials from past investors to share to a potential financier of their next movie will put them further ahead than if they had no testimonials to begin with.

- **Electronic Press Kits:** An electronic press kit (EPK) is a pre-packaged set of promotional materials providing information about a company, project, organization, or person, with the purpose of it being distributed to a member of the media for promotional use. For an independent film, press kits include biographies of the filmmakers, cast members, and important crew, along with photos, images, and behind-the-scenes footage of the project. A short and long synopsis of the screenplay, statements from the producers or directors, and any noteworthy press coverage are also found in a movie EPK. If the film won any sort of awards at either a domestic or international film festival, you should also include this information as well. Keep in mind, most film festivals even require you include a press kit in your submission. When submitted to the media by either you or a publicist, individual journalists will take your press kit and use it as a guide to write their coverage. If you have generated any sort of media coverage, whether it's through a local newspaper, national magazine, or a regional news channel, you should always display links on your website or directly send them to your prospect if it makes sense.

- **Comparative Analysis:** Another helpful sales material a filmmaker can use is an analysis highlighting elements like budgets and revenue projections of their film compared with other, similarly produced movies in the marketplace. The more elements you can match, including genre, actors, and story plots, the better. Using websites like IMDbPro and The-numbers.com, a filmmaker can take this information and ultimately present it to financiers, sales agents, and distributors to articulate their project's potential in the marketplace compared with other equivalent titles. When putting together a comparative analysis of your project, keep in mind that you should only list films released within the past few years. Trying to compare a film released in 1978 with a film in 2020 will not work, as a result of many elements, including great advances in technology, avenues of distribution, and more.

Value Demonstration Summary

Most of the time when people think of sales, they think about the act of persuading someone to make a decision or take a particular action. Although convincing or persuading someone is a major part of the sales process, demonstrating one's value of themselves, their project, or service is how successful salespeople get their prospect's buy-in. Being considered an expert in your field, employing storytelling to connect with your prospects, and building sales collateral to reinforce value are all significant ways to demonstrate the advantages of your offering.

Despite being a billionaire and one of America's most successful business magnates, Bill Gates continues to read fifty books a year to expand his knowledge. No matter how old you are and how much experience you think you have, it's never too late to continue learning. As an independent filmmaker, taking the knowledge you have accumulated from methods like books, education, hands-on experience, and imparting this knowledge in your daily conversations with the people around you will only help you in building credibility and sealing a deal.

Since storytelling and filmmaking already go hand-in-hand, it's a matter of using storytelling in your personal conversations to convey emotion and build a connection with your audience. Providing your unique voice while simultaneously keeping your prospect genuinely interested will only help you in your attempts to articulate the value of yourself, your project, or your service.

Lastly, developing an arsenal of sales collateral to provide your prospect with visual references conveying what you and your offering can bring to the table will only help make the case on why your prospect should proceed. Whether it's a comprehensive business plan for investors to see how their money will be spent on your project or a vibrant movie pitch deck to generate excitement among your cast and crew, these materials will further move you along in exemplifying the merits of your opportunity.

CHAPTER 6
DEMONSTRATE VALUE—
A CASE STUDY

Demonstrating Value to the Financier

If the act of asking an individual for a large sum of money so you can get your film made doesn't seem like a sales pursuit to you, I'm not sure what is. It takes money to get projects made, and without it, filmmakers will find themselves at a dead-end. As an independent filmmaker, it's very unlikely you will be able to knock on the studio gates of Fox and Paramount and ask them to let you borrow a few hundred thousand dollars so you can make your low-budget action-adventure film. So where does a filmmaker go to find money for their movie?

The first place you can start looking is your personal network. This includes everyone, from your close friends and family members to co-workers. If anyone is most likely to happily hand over their cash so you can make your movie, it's Aunt Barbara and your second cousin Bill. Were you in a sorority or fraternity in college? Does one of your friend's family members invest in interesting opportunities? Every chance you get to tell someone about your project you should give them your high-level elevator pitch. Pull out a piece of paper and jot down all the people who are connected to you, along with the people connected to them.

Other places you can try are associations and organizations. If your film touches on a specific topic like depression or anxiety, you can reach out to organizations focusing on mental health awareness. If your documentary focuses on the negative impacts of animal cruelty, you can reach out to animal rights groups that share a common value. There are plenty of grants available from these organizations, but in addition to grant opportunities, reaching out and generating interest from the individual members of these groups can lead to private investments.

Lastly, think about all the top-paying jobs there are in the world. Lawyers, dentists, doctors, and engineers often have hefty salaries and sometimes have so much money they don't know what to do with. Using online prospecting tools like lead-generation services and spider programs that collect the contact information of high net-worth individuals based on their job titles is a great way for you to build an email list of potential investors. Engineers spend their days calculating mind-numbing equations and reading code. Being able to tell their family and friends they're investing in a comedy movie would put smiles on their faces and give them something exciting to talk about!

Keep in mind that when it comes to raising money for your project, you should always consult the legal advice of an attorney. There are many Securities and Exchange Commission (SEC) laws in place that independent filmmakers must abide by. To play it safe, you want to make sure you put together what is called a private placement memorandum (PPM). A PPM is a legal document provided to prospective investors when offering stock or another security in a business. A lawyer will walk you through the process of creating a limited liability corporation (LLC) for your project, along with ensuring the language in your PPM abides by SEC regulations. Whatever you do, do not attempt to create your own PPM by taking a template you find off the internet. There are endless potential legal risks that can occur and aren't worth the headache.

With so many available options to get financing for your next movie, how does a filmmaker convey the value of their project to a potential investor? What specific methods can they use to communicate their project's value? This hypothetical case study on the demonstrate value stage is centered on the creation of a pitch deck, one of the most important sales materials a filmmaker will need to effectively express the vision of the project and ultimately acquire an investment from a prospective financier.

Pitch Deck Goals

As mentioned in the previous chapter, a pitch deck is a high-level presentation introducing your film in a visual form. Most importantly, pitch decks are tangible. It's something a financier can touch and feel with their own hands while also being able to consume an optical representation of your film. In theory, a pitch deck is your sales capability deck for your project. Pitch decks have three main goals:

- Selling the idea of your project in a visually appealing way

- Demonstrating the value(s) of your project and gearing appropriate value(s) to specific audiences

- Fleshing out the script and your ideas into one centralized document

Pitch Deck Elements

Depending on who you are speaking to, your pitch deck will consist of specific pieces demonstrating the value to your audience. For example, a pitch deck geared to a cinematographer will consist of visual references, locations, and compatible films. A pitch deck for an investor, on the other hand, will consist of cast and crew biographies, synopsis of the screenplay, marketing and distribution strategies, and more. Since one of the goals of your pitch deck is to demonstrate value to your prospect, you must initially ask yourself: *What would my prospect find valuable?*

Here are a few major elements one would find in a conventional independent film pitch deck presented to a prospective financier:

Title Page

The title page is the first slide of your presentation. It's the first thing your prospect is going to see, and it's going to make either a good or bad impression on them whether you like it or not. The goal of your title page is to introduce the title of your project and provide readers with a sense of the visual style. Your title's logo is a very important tool when it comes to expressing the tone and look of your film. For example, if your film has dark and mysterious themes, you can convey this with a classic noir-styled font. If your family comedy takes place in Hawaii, a fun and vibrant tropical font might be the best choice.

Another element to think about is the title page background. Do you want it to be a photo of someone or something? A type of pattern? A specific color or colors? Keep in mind, the last thing you want to do is overwhelm your reader with a cluttered first page with a bunch of text and multiple images. Since first impressions are very important, keeping your title page simple will always do the trick.

Disclaimer

Since you are presenting your pitch deck to potential investors, for legal purposes it's important to ensure the document does not offer to sell or solicit an offer to buy securities or any other investment instrument. Your private placement memorandum (PPM) would be considered the appropriate document to offer these investment opportunities for your project. As mentioned earlier, you want to ensure you are abiding by SEC regulations and not raising money in an illegal manner. Including a disclaimer that states the intended purpose of your pitch deck will ensure your reader is fully aware of your intentions and direct the appropriate people to your PPM if they are interested in learning more about how they can invest.

You also should include a statement on confidentiality in the disclaimer section of your pitch deck. State that your materials are for the confidential use of the party to whom it was provided and how your reader may not reproduce your content or distribute it to other parties without your consent. This is because the last thing you want is your reader sending your pitch deck all over town without your permission. The disclaimer section is an essential part of your pitch deck to legally protect yourself and your project.

Log Line

A log line is a brief summary of your project, communicating the protagonist, central conflict of the story, and an emotional "hook" to generate interest from your reader. How does one take 120 pages of a screenplay and condense it into one or two sentences? There are plenty of resources that go over the many elements that make up a successful log line, but here are the major points to keep in mind when creating a log line for your project:

- **Use General Log Line Structure:** A way to identify your story's protagonist, their goal, inciting incident, major conflict, and main stakes is to use general log line structure found in a majority of log lines:

  When **INCITING INCIDENT OCCURS…**

  A **CHARACTER TYPE…**

  Must **OBJECTIVE…**

  Before **STAKES.**

- **Stay Within 25 to 50 Words:** Refrain from being too wordy and meticulous. The whole point of the log line is to effectively articulate your story in a clear and concise format to generate interest from your audience to ultimately read the entire screenplay. Remember, the simpler the better!

- **Read Other Log Lines:** Check out some of the log lines of your favorite movies on websites like IMDb. Look at the log lines of similar movies to the one you are making. Pay close attention to how they describe the central conflict and emotional hook of the story.

- **Avoid Character Names:** You want to focus more on character types rather than character names. If your main character is a struggling single mother or an alcoholic stock broker, including this information in your log line will also create instant conflict context for the reader.

- **Write Multiple Options:** You're never going to get the log line perfect on your first attempt. Since writing is all about rewriting, attempt to create at least ten to fifteen options of your log line. Experiment with different wording, structure, and elements to see which one you like the best.

Artist Statement

Whether it's the director, writer, or one of the producers on your project, your pitch deck should include a very compelling statement on why this film should be made. There are so many other stories out there that can be made into movies, but what sets this story apart from the others? Artist statements uncover why the filmmakers are passionate about bringing this story to life.

Another piece of information you want to include is what the target audience is for your project. Will your film resonate with women between the ages of 25 and 35, or would anyone over the age of 40 appreciate it? Take a look at similar movies in the marketplace and see what target audiences it connected with. If your film is a science fiction horror with teenage protagonists, it's most likely not going to play very well with an elderly audience. Outlining your project's key demographic will demonstrate your knowledge of your product and will also convince investors you have done your homework.

Lastly, how is your director going to take the story's subject matter and translate it on screen? What's their unique take on the genre, characters, and locations? A director can highlight some of the shooting styles they plan on implementing, along with the overall visual aesthetics of color and tone they plan on using. Even if you are a first-time director, the artist statement is a way for you to communicate why this project is special to you, the methods you will use in telling the story, what you hope for audiences to experience, and more.

Comparable Films

What better way to communicate the value of your project than listing similar movies in the marketplace that have seen success? Comparative analysis of other films can be considered an entirely other sales material exhibiting the benefits of your project. Provide two or three comparable films that have been made and released in the past few years and are similar to your project in both scale and scope. If you are making a low-budget character-driven drama, select other similar films following a protagonist and were made with a limited budget.

You can choose to include each film's log line, budget, and their return on investment as well. Keep in mind, since you are making an independent film, that it might be hard to find films sharing the same budget. It will also be extremely hard to be able to identify return on investment numbers for those films. Try the best you can to put together this data. However, if for some reason you aren't able to locate the correct information, do not put generalizations or flat out lie. Your readers and especially potential investors will do their own research, and they won't be happy if your lies are exposed. There's no doubt someone will have reservations about giving you money if you attempt to lie to them. Remember, you want to establish trust and credibility and demonstrate value to your prospect.

Synopsis

You already included your project's log line earlier in the pitch deck. Why must you also include a detailed synopsis of the story? It's because you want to provide your reader with a better understanding of your main character, the conflicts involved, and what the overall story arc is. A synopsis is a summary of your story that familiarizes your reader with the plot and how it unfolds.

Since one of the goals of the pitch deck is to flesh out the screenplay and your ideas into one centralized document, adding a synopsis will paint a clearer picture so your reader can fully understand the other elements, such as the characters, production design, locations, and more, in your deck. Without a general understanding of some of the events taking place in your story, how would you expect a reader to be able to fully comprehend the profiles of your supporting characters?

Your synopsis should only be around 250 to 300 words. Enough to be able to describe who the protagonist is, what their main challenge and motivations are, and the many obstacles they experience in their journey to complete the story arc. Keep in mind, you want to include essential story elements like the inciting incident, rising action, midpoint, and climax to effectively convey the story's arc. You may want to leave out the resolution of the story, to spark enough interest from your readers to ultimately read the full screenplay. Using the same process that created your log line, write a few versions of your synopsis using different wording and arrangement of elements. When you are done, you should edit out unnecessary words and make sure everything flows. It's always helpful to get the feedback from others on how your synopsis reads and how it can be improved.

Visual Reference

Your pitch deck is a sales tool that communicates the value of your movie; and because a movie is a visual art form, it only makes sense to include a representation of your intended visual style. Visual elements like shooting techniques, color palettes, and aspect ratio and framing are all examples of ways you can communicate your project's visual style. Sit down with the director and cinematographer of your project and inquire about their personal take on the visual style. Take all the elements of the visual aesthetics you, your director, and your cinematographer have created and try to summarize it in one slide of your pitch deck.

You should also include a slide devoted to images from other films, television shows, and other media closely resembling your project's summary on visual style. Think about other films you have watched that share a similar tone and setting. If you stated your film has a dark and eerie vibe, think about other movies or television shows that share the same feeling. This will allow your reader, including your prospective financier, to envision how your movie will look before you even click the RECORD button on a camera. More important, adding a visual reference will make your project more real and palpable.

Locations

Sometimes the location where your story takes place is as important as your story's protagonist. If your film revolves around a group of college kids stranded at a bed and breakfast in a deep rural section of Iowa, the location of the film will play a key part in the movie's overall look and feel. This is especially true for films that take place in only one or two locations or films that take place twenty years ago. If your film is a period piece set in the 1960s, what kind of locations do you have access to or plan to get access to that complement a 1960s energy? Go through your script and try to identify some prominent and unique locations to include in your pitch deck.

Providing a picture collage of multiple locations will provide your reader with an even greater sense of how your film will look. Locations have personalities of their own through elements like architecture, Mother Nature, crowd control, and more. Any way you can illustrate these distinctive elements in your sales presentation will elevate your story. Sometimes you might find yourself talking to a reader, especially a potential investor, who grew up where you planned to shoot and who can help you with introductions to some of these shooting locations, along with other resources benefitting the production.

Production Design

Production design includes everything from designed film sets, locations, props, and wardrobe. Every visual element located in the film
and how those elements work together to create a world on screen
that complements the project's overall visual style. Colors, themes,
compositions, and other elements that work in tandem with each
other to evoke the emotions, themes, and actions of each character
and scene are the core essence of what production design is all about.

In your pitch deck you want to include some images of the significant props, wardrobe, makeup, and film sets found in your project.
If your film takes place in 1980, share some photos of props and
clothing your characters will be using. If your protagonist rides a
specific type of bicycle throughout the entire film, establish what this
bicycle looks like. If your protagonist wears excessive makeup and
has a bizarre sense of clothing style, include a few visual references.
Any physical item directly connecting to your protagonist's state of
mind should also be included. For example, if your protagonist has
very antiquated ideals and is living in the modern world, you can
express this through the faded and outdated wallpaper and furniture
in her house. Like the other element sections of your pitch deck,
such as locations and visual references, the whole point is to further
communicate the look and feel of your film.

Character Breakdowns

Your protagonist isn't the only essential character in your story. It also
consists of a variety of supporting characters who help your protagonist along the way in their journey. Dorothy from the *Wizard of Oz*
is a notable character, but how about the Lion, Tin Woodman, and
the Scarecrow. They had their own significant personal agendas all
while contributing to Dorothy's goal of going home. Dorothy even
has an antagonist, the Wicked Witch of the West, whose goal is to
make sure Dorothy doesn't get home. In your pitch deck you want to
include breakdowns of your story's leading role and every character
you believe to be a major contributor to your protagonist's endeavors.

The breakdown of your protagonist should only be about 250 to 500 words, while your supporting character breakdowns should only be about 100 to 300 words each. When creating your breakdowns, think about areas of your characters' lives that you believe would be helpful for your reader to understand them better. How are the characters related to your protagonist? Where does each character fit in the story, and what significant events unfold while they are present? What are their personal conflicts? Highlighting physical, emotional, and other traits of your characters will give readers a fuller picture of who they are and how they fit into the story. For example, a "smarmy used car salesman who still carries on like he's an eighteen-year-old frat boy" will convey the character's true essence better than "used car salesman."

Creative Team Biographies

One of the most strategic ways to prove to your audience that you and your team are the best people to bring this project to fruition is by including biographies highlighting relevant work experience, education, and backgrounds. Ultimately these biographies should capture why any potential investor should trust you and your team to get the job done.

Think about all the relevant work experiences you have had in the past relating to your ability to successfully complete this film. Some examples would include producing five other feature films in the past, working at a production company for two years, or recently completing an internship with a distribution company. The same goes for your educational background. Did you get a bachelor's degree in your field from a prestigious university? Lastly, any sort of relevant awards and recognitions should be included in your biography. If one of your short films won a best film award at a film festival or if you acquired domestic and international distribution on your last project, you should include this in your overview.

The core creative team should consist of main producers, the director, and screenwriter. Each biography should only be about 250 to 500 words and should also include a professional headshot of the person placed directly next to the biography. A prospective financier will feel more confident if they discover the core creative team has had some initial experience. Even if you don't have experience under your belt, it's all about how you present your background in a way that will persuade your competence for the project. If you strongly feel like you don't have enough experience under your belt to secure enough investment, think about attaching an industry veteran to your project. Not only will the industry professional's experience impress your investors, they will also provide immense guidance and value to the project.

Social Themes and Topics

If your film touches on a group of social themes or topics your audience might be able to connect with, it's advantageous to include a slide outlining their importance. Additionally, by outlining the social themes and topics of your project, you are establishing why they need to be exhibited. For example, if your film explores feminism, child abuse, and depression, touching on their significance and implications they have on our society will further your ability to demonstrate the value of your project.

If you are showing your pitch deck to individuals with the hopes of securing funding for your project, outlining these social themes and topics will also help you in understanding the appropriate groups of people and organizations to potentially target. For example, if your protagonist has been abused as a child and this plays a huge role in the challenges they are facing, you should make a targeted email list of organizations with the mission of stopping child abuse. These organizations also have individual members who might understand the value of your project solely based on the exploration of topics they are passionate about.

In your pitch deck you want to list a few outstanding statistics surrounding the social theme or topic. For instance, for a project about child abuse, you can include: "2.9 million cases of child abuse are reported every year in the United States." By doing this you are taking your project's social theme and amplifying its importance.

Knowing that 2.9 million children are abused each year in the United States will demonstrate to your reader why your message needs to be told to the world.

Contact Information and Thank You

On the last page of your pitch deck you want to include your contact information, including your or your company's phone number, email address, and website. Providing your contact information will convey that you are the real deal and not some fly-by-night operation to raise money for an imaginary film. If you don't have a website for your project or film production company yet, it might be a good time to get started before you reach out to potential investors.

Lastly, it's important to provide a quick "Thank you for your time and consideration" slide for taking the time to read your pitch deck. Your prospective investors are constantly bombarded with an array of financial investment pitches. Sometimes showing a little gratitude goes a long way. Lastly, you should state that if they are in need of further documents, including your PPM, to directly reach out to you and you will provide the location where they can access the collateral.

Case Study—A Final Word on Demonstrating Value

Having the appropriate sales materials to show a prospective investor will either result in a written check or a finger point to the door. Demonstrating your project's value by creating a comprehensive pitch deck of your film will guarantee your ability to establish trustworthiness with about any financier. Before you pick up the phone and dial your uncle's rich best friend Dale, take the time to carefully craft a vigorous proposal highlighting every element of your film, including character breakdowns, creative biographies, production design, social themes, and more.

When dealing with prospective investors, remember they are real people like you and me. You have no reason to be intimidated or nervous because you know in your heart your project is of direct value to them. Having done your due diligence on this individual in the discovery stage, you have confidently recognized ways your project will benefit them and even potentially solve their roadblocks. Keep in mind, as much as you want their investment, whatever you do, refrain from overpromising on things you realistically cannot deliver. Use your best judgment and don't offer to introduce your financier to Steven Spielberg or Tom Cruise if you don't have relationships with them. Genuinely show interest in your investor and their background and identify other ways you can provide value to them. Whether it's letting one of their kids be an extra in a scene or introducing your investor to your lead actress, think of things they would appreciate. As much as you want full creative control on your project, you need to realize you might need to negotiate on a few areas since you are using other people's money.

Demonstrating value happens in many forms. Whether it's through developing knowledge of your product or service, using storytelling to convey favorable outcomes, or building sales materials that reinforce utility, an independent filmmaker needs to ask herself or himself, "What's the best way to make my case?" A producer getting buy-in for investment in their feature film from a conference room full of investors, a freelance cinematographer persuading a director to give him a shot, and a screenwriter trying to land a powerful literary agent are all cases where demonstrating value is imperative.

STAGE IV

CLOSING THE DEAL

CHAPTER 7
CLOSING THE DEAL

Defining Deal Closing

At this juncture in the sales process, you have thoroughly researched your prospect, held a discovery call to identify their goals and pain points, and demonstrated the value of your project or service. Now it's time for what is on every salesperson's mind: the firm handshake, the swipe of a credit card, or the wet ink signature on a contract. It's time to officially close the deal.

As the fourth stage of the sales process, deal closing is where agreements are finalized, money has been transferred, and most importantly, where business relationships truly begin. It's a time where every salesperson feels validated for all the hard work they have put in up to this point. You have done a good job in conveying the merits of your project or service, but you are not officially done yet.

Deal Closing Goals

In the deal closing phase of the sales process it's vitally important you are:

- Handling any of your prospect's objections and eliminating any sort of fears

- Asking for their business and invoking a sense of urgency

- Establishing your agreement in writing with a legally binding contract

Deal Closing Steps

When it comes to closing a deal, there are four major steps: addressing any of your prospect's remaining objections or fears, directly asking for the sale, invoking a sense of urgency, and getting your business agreement in writing.

Step #1: Handle Objections

The last thing people want to hear is the word "no." There is no doubt that rejection is a tough pill to swallow, and salespeople across the world would rather jump off a bridge than hear the letters N-O come out of their prospect's mouth.

An objection is an explicit expression by a prospect that indicates some sort of barrier exists between what the salesperson has pitched so far and what needs to be satisfied before fully getting the prospect's buy-in. Contrary to popular belief, an objection is a good indication your prospect is engaged and is candidly considering your proposal.

When your prospect indicates they are not ready to move forward with your proposition, whatever you do, do not be discouraged. Handling objections is a part of the process, whether we like it or not.

In the sphere of independent filmmaking, you might hear objections like: "I'm not interested in your project," or "I don't have time on my schedule to be there for production," or "I'm not in need of your services right now." Don't be disheartened. To get your prospect closer to the sale, you must listen to, acknowledge, respond, and validate their objections (LARV):

- **Listen:** The first thing you most likely think about doing when someone rejects you is to immediately respond to them and defend your position. However, you should resist the temptation to do so. When you jump right in and respond too quickly, you jeopardize making assumptions about the objection. Instead of reacting defensively, use your listening skills to fully understand the prospect's concerns without bias; and most importantly, make sure your body language is communicating your openness to listen with purpose. No one likes being interrupted, especially when they are voicing their concerns. By taking a deep breath and fully listening to your prospect, you are showing you are concerned with their best interests in mind.

- **Acknowledge:** The objections your prospect vocalizes may not be the true underlying issues stopping them from moving forward. As a salesperson, it's your job to get to the core of your prospect's objections and ultimately understand them in a full capacity. In order to do this, you must ask for your prospect's approval in allowing them to fully understand and investigate the issues they have outlined. Once you've inspected the concerns they have shared with you, it's crucial you restate the objection back to them. This way your prospect will hear their problem being communicated back to them, and you as a salesperson can get closer to the root of the objection. Digging deeper into their objections by asking follow-up questions ("Why...?" "How...?" and "What else...?") will encourage your prospect to let down their barrier and reveal what's stopping them from closing a deal with you.

- **Respond:** As soon as you feel like you have uncovered every possible objection from your prospect and shown your ability to fully understand them, you should begin to address them by responding to the prospect's biggest objection first. Your goal is to resolve all their fears and reservations as quickly as possible. However, if you feel like you don't have all the answers at your fingertips to be able to solve one of their main issues, it's best to make sure you don't try to wing it. Do whatever you need to do to access the information to successfully address their problem. Your prospect wasn't born yesterday and will sniff out half-assed answers in a heartbeat. Make sure you don't lose your credibility by choosing to lie to them so close to the finish line.

■ **Validate:** After you have confidently responded to all of your prospect's objections, you should confirm your answers have satisfied all of their doubts. Go one step further and ask them if they are happy with your responses to their objections and proceed to quickly list the value propositions of your project or service. Sometimes you will find a prospect needs some more time to think about your proposal. Do not be a slimy used car salesman and attempt to pressure them into making a decision right away. You have enough faith in the value of your offering and you know your prospect will come around and make the right decision.

Here are some of the most common objections prospects share and tips on how to handle them:

Price

A screenwriter not being okay with the price a producer offered on their script, an investor not willing to part with a certain amount of money, and a producer not willing to open their budget to pay more for a cinematographer. These are all examples of price objections found in independent filmmaking. Whether it's because what you are asking for is too much or too little, the trick of overcoming these types of objections is to reiterate the value your prospect is getting from your project or service and how it's ultimately worth the price. Attempt to find out what's really going on and if money is the reason your prospect doesn't want to move forward. Brainstorm ways your prospect can allocate a budget out of their funds to contribute to your project or service. If you are offering less in monetary payment to your prospect, think about other ways your project or service is providing solutions to their pain points and goals.

Fit

An actress not believing the role is right for her, a director not approving a cinematographer's camera package, and an owner worried about how a movie will be shot in his restaurant. These objections center on how your project or service doesn't make sense for them, is too hard to deal with, or it's not for them. The way to handle these types of objections is to gain a better understanding of what's keeping your prospect back. You should also outline their pain points and goals they have shared in the discovery phase and proceed to connect to how your project or service can directly benefit them.

Interest

A distributor not wanting to acquire a filmmaker's movie, a director already happy with the editor they have always worked with, and a local band not wanting to let a producer use their music in his film. The general brushoff is a common objection but very simple to counter. When an individual tells you outright they are not interested in what you are offering, it means they have ruminated on one reason why it's not necessary to move forward with you. The best way to counter these types of objections is to persuade them to change their perspective on the one reason why they don't want to move forward. Of course, the first step is being able to identify what the reason is, which you can do by asking probing questions.

Time

A financier not having the time to go over your business plan, a producer who hasn't read a writer's script yet, and a potential client who doesn't need video services at the moment. People have all sorts of commitments in their daily life, and we of course cannot expect them to drop everything they are doing to accommodate us. To deal with this type of objection, one must continue to casually follow up with their prospect. Whether it's once a week or once every few weeks, be sure to stay on your prospect's radar. Have a variety of follow-up email templates handy to send out. Be sure to provide new information or updates in each follow-up to refrain from repeating yourself. If trying to schedule a discovery call with them, assure your prospect it will only take thirty minutes out of their day and it will be worth their time.

Gatekeeper

An actor having to talk to their agent or manager, a potential client having to ask their boss for approval, and an acquisition executive needing to talk to the rest of the team. Gatekeepers are living and breathing objections standing in the way of you being able to sign an agreement. Instead of looking at gatekeepers as a roadblock, aim to develop trust with them over time and demonstrate the value of your project or service like you did to the original prospect you spoke to. Sharing specific examples of how your project or service will benefit your prospect to the gatekeeper will aid in making your case. Always confirm with your prospect if there is anyone else responsible in the decision-making process. If there is, ask for the gatekeeper's contact information and get in touch with them directly.

Competition

A production that has already secured a sound editor, a client who is already working with another production company, and a distributor who already acquired a film similar to yours. These objections are typically the hardest to combat but not impossible. It's entirely possible your competitor is offering more advanced features and a cheaper price. However, confidently expressing why your project or service is superior to other options is a way to change your prospect's mind. If they say they are happy with their current solution, ask them to explain the reasons why they are pleased. Be sure to fully listen to them and communicate how your solution would be an even better fit for them. If you have enough knowledge about your competitor, you can identify areas where they fall short and, in turn, promote how your project or service will make a mark.

Hard No

Receiving a hard no can happen in about any scenario in independent filmmaking. Although it might be hard to find the motivation to keep pressing on, you must continue to do so. Sales is all about persistence, and the fact that you believe in what you are offering means there is no reason why your prospect should not move forward. Think about how many people usually retreat after hearing an initial rejection from someone. If they choose to power through and continue to convince a person, they may find that they get what they ask for. Don't be that person who looks back at their life and wishes they had tried harder. Even if you get hung up on, screw up the courage to call the person right back. Don't take anything personally, and remember how much value your project or service can provide to your prospect.

One final note on objection handling is to keep track of every objection you receive. Write these objections down in a notebook, on your phone, or your computer. List every objection along with a well-crafted response. You can also proactively think of all the potential objections you may receive from a distributor, financier, producer, location manager, or others. Write your answers to these objections, keeping in mind to connect their pain points and goals to the value of your solution.

Step #2: Ask for the Sale

One of the biggest reasons a salesperson doesn't land a deal is because they did not ask the prospect for their commitment. Every time you leave a call or a meeting with a prospect without gaining commitment, the odds of you securing a commitment later are reduced by 50 percent. Having already done so much work in identifying the prospect's pain points and goals and demonstrating the value of their offering, salespeople often don't ask for the sale because they beat around the bush. Reluctance to close can be frustrating, but you must realize this reluctance is self-induced.

There are a variety of reasons why salespeople fail to ask for the sale, including the following:

- **Fear of Rejection:** This is one of the main reasons the general population stays out of sales in the first place. Nobody likes to get rejected. However, Wayne Gretzky can remind us that we miss 100 percent of the shots we don't take. If you don't at least attempt to shoot your shot, you will never truly know. If your prospect says no to you, it doesn't mean they are rejecting you as a person. It means they are not ready to make a commitment on your project or service at the moment. Remember not to take anything personally.

- **Lack of Confidence:** If you aren't sold on your project or service yourself, how do you expect others to be sold on it? Lacking the confidence in your own solution is another reason why most salespeople don't ask for the sale. One effective way of overcoming this is to ask yourself how your offering will benefit your prospect. After hearing what's important to your prospect, you should be able to have a solid understanding of how your project or service will provide value to them.

- **Fear of Threatening the Relationship:** Everyone wants to be liked by their peers. A strong relationship will ultimately increase your influence because your prospect values your advice and expertise. However, some salespeople might confuse this relationship with their client for friendship. They are afraid that by doing business with this person they will ultimately jeopardize their friendship, which can't be further from the truth. Individuals want to be in business with people they like and respect. Prospects understand your goal is eventually asking them for commitment, and they expect you to ask them.

- **Unsure of When to Ask:** You don't want to ask too early to avoid coming off too pushy, and if you ask too late you might miss the opportunity. The best time to ask for commitment is after your prospect has shared information about their goals and problems and you have demonstrated the value your project or service can provide. This is because you established that you listened to them and offered them a solution tailored to their needs. Also, pay attention to positive commitment signals from your prospect. If they are asking questions on the best way to send the money, contracts they need to sign, or any other form of next steps, it means they are most likely committed.

■ **Unsure of How to Ask:** There are many awkward ways to ask for someone's commitment. Whether it's asking a financier to finally write a check or asking a client to hire your production company for their upcoming event, you don't want to come off too pushy. One of the best ways to ask your prospect for their commitment is to ask them an assumptive closing question. These questions assume your prospect has already agreed with moving forward. For example, "Whose contact information should I put on the contract?" or "Would it be easier for you to send the check in the mail?" or "How does next Tuesday work for you to get started on everything?"

Closing Phrases

Sometimes it makes sense to strategically use distinctive closing phrases or pose certain types of questions during scenarios where you need to ask for the sale. There are a few different types of closing techniques when asking for the sale, whether it's closing a prospect with an assumptive question or a hard statement.

Here are five closing techniques and phrases to use when asking for the sale:

■ **Synopsis Close:** Reiterate what your prospect is signing up for or purchasing, all while simultaneously stressing the value and benefits. It will not only demonstrate how you have listened to the prospect and genuinely took the time to identify solutions, it also reminds your prospect of the exciting opportunity you are pitching to them. For example, my cinematography services include the shoot, along with my camera and lighting equipment I already own. I also have both a first and second camera assistant included in my quote. "Since your shoot is fairly soon, when would be a good time for me to start planning?"

- **Sharp Angle Close:** Your prospect is in the business of sales as much as you are. They will attempt to try to negotiate price reductions, add-ons, and everything else under the sun. They know they have the upper hand, so it's no skin off their back to at least try. If you have approval to accommodate their request, you should respond with, "Sure. However, if I do this for you, can we get started with everything today?" Sharp angle closing phrases can be used when asked for additional requested perks by an actress, director, financier, and more.

- **Query Close:** You've been asking questions since the very beginning. You might as well close the deal with a question as well. Query closes allow you to identify anything standing in the way of you and your prospect coming to an agreement. For example, a producer asking a screenwriter "Is there anything holding you back from letting me option the script from you?" means the producer is either going to get closure or more information as to what is holding the screenwriter back from moving forward.

- **Assumptive Close:** Positive thinking makes all the difference. You must believe in your project or service and feel like there is no reason why your prospect should not think the same. Monitor how your prospect engages and objects throughout your presentation to them. Are they convinced as well? Are they suspicious about something? By paying close attention you will have a good feeling if they feel the same way as you. One example of an assumptive closing question is, say, a producer asking a screenwriter, "What's the best address to send your option agreement check to?"

- **Silky Close:** The silky close is the complete opposite of the hard close. It's a method of showing your prospect the benefits of your project or service, followed up with a low-impact question to identify if they would be open to learning more. If a film editor is told by a potential client they already have an editor for their project, they can proceed to ask them, "If I reduced your current post-production schedule and cut your post-production budget in half, all while creating an extraordinary final cut, would you be interested in learning more?" How can a prospect not want to learn more? It would be extremely hard for them to turn down a discussion centered on potentially cutting their project's timeline and expenses in half.

Step #3: Invoke Urgency

Invoking a sense of urgency to close a deal is a successful way to get your prospect to act quickly and get the agreement signed and the money in the bank. However, your objective is to get your prospect to make a decision, all while not coming off like a pushy used car salesman or, worse, a scam artist. Prospects have their own needs and timelines, which are more important to them than what you may be offering them. How does one go about invoking a sense of urgency without coming on too strong?

- **Build Urgency from the Beginning of the Sales Process:** Communicate that you are on a set timeline as early as your first conversation with them. A producer who is looking to make their next project and be in pre-production by April will let a screenwriter know they can't sit around and think about the option agreement offered for their screenplay.

- **Move Up Next Step Dates:** Instead of asking a financier to reconnect in the next few weeks to present your business plan in detail, why not insist on meeting with them in a few days? If your prospect suggests a later date, recommend something sooner. Be sure to be polite about it and not come off as too aggressive. You will find most of the time they will agree to your request.

■ **Refocus on the Pain Points Your Project or Service Solves:** If your prospect has shared that they are running out of time and need to get production started as soon as possible, refocus on how you and your services can step in and solve this problem for them right away. Remind them that the longer they wait, the longer their pain points continue and the longer they don't achieve their goals. Showing them all the negative consequences of not working with you should make them realize how much they need you.

■ **Offer an Incentive:** Incentives can include anything from money, time, resources, physical goods, and more. If an actress is on the fence about playing the role, offer them something that will sweeten the deal. You also want to establish an end date for when this additional incentive will expire. This will light a fire under them to quickly make a decision.

■ **Establish Scarcity:** If you are shown to be a hot commodity, everyone in town will want you; but if there's too much of you available, it will turn people off. This is because your value increases when you are perceived to be popular. If you're a freelance filmmaker in the middle of negotiations with a prospective client, let them know you have a jam-packed schedule and suggest they make a decision sooner rather than later or else someone else will book you. Watch how fast your prospect will lock you down.

Step #4: Get It in Writing

A contract is a document that recognizes and governs the rights and obligations of the parties outlined in an agreement. Although I highly suggest consulting with a lawyer when drafting any form of legal agreement, by no means does this mean you can't have a starting point by drafting a basic agreement yourself. With so many online legal resources for filmmakers available, including contract templates, there's no reason why you shouldn't have an agreement in writing.

Whether you are offering a role to an actress, securing crew members for your production, or signing a distribution agreement, as an independent filmmaker it's in your best interest to get the negotiated deal in writing and signed by both parties. There are too many horror stories of film projects crumbling to disaster because two people were unable to work out differences. If only they had recorded an agreement outlining every aspect of the business relationship, there most likely would not have been any sort of contention.

They are plenty of reasons, but here are the top five reasons why it's imperative to have your agreement in writing:

1. **Helps Minimize Disputes or Issues:** In the world of filmmaking, anything can happen; and you can plan for problems to occur. Although a contract won't ensure problems won't occur, it can help minimize them. Having a contract will encourage both parties to cooperate and attempt to fix the issue rather than paying expensive legal fees.

2. **Limits Liability:** Outlining in a contract what you are responsible for and what you are not responsible for will solidify expectations and ensure the other party can't come after you. For example, if a producer specifically states in a talent agreement that they aren't responsible for the actress's health while off set any time during production, they are protecting themselves if something unfortunate happens to her.

3. **Helps Build Trust and Transparency:** Nothing expresses that you are a person of your word more than insisting on having your statements in writing. Having a contract in place will establish a sense of trust that you are someone who is committed in delivering what they propose. Not having a contract would make you look sketchy and suggest you are someone who thinks he can easily get away with not fulfilling obligations.

4. **Helps Gets You Paid:** Money is a big part of the equation when it comes to business. We all need to get paid so we can pay our bills and comfortably enjoy our lives. A contract can communicate when and how you or your prospect will get paid. It also can outline the total amount for services rendered in case you need to verify this information at some point in the future.

5. **Protects Intellectual Property:** Whether it's protecting a screen-play or the confidentiality centered on your project, intellectual property is a valuable asset, and you want to do everything you can to safeguard it. Having intellectual property outlined in an agreement will clarify any misunderstandings centered on the ownership of the documents.

Now that you can see why having a contract is so important when it comes to closing a deal, you must now ask yourself what particular areas you need to include to ensure both parties are protected. The answer is: it depends. It depends on who you are making the agreement with and the nature of the deal you are setting in place. A contract outlining the relationship between a producer and a distributor will look a whole lot different from a contract between a producer and an actress or key grip.

I also highly recommend checking out the book *Hollywood Dealmaking: Negotiating Talent Agreements for Film, TV, and New Media* by Dina Appleton and Daniel Yankelevits. Also check out entertainment lawyer Mark Litwak's website Marklitwak.com to order 80 downloadable contract templates for all types of agreements.

Deal Closing Summary

Taking the advice of Alec Baldwin's character in the classic film *Glengarry Glen Ross,* it goes without saying that salespeople should always be closing. However, deal closing isn't what most people think it is. The accurate way to close deals is through problem solving and providing value. One should always avoid hard selling techniques, as they have proven to be extremely ineffective with prospects. Closing a deal and finalizing an agreement is a major cornerstone in the process of sales that ensures the salesperson addresses any of the prospect's objections, asks the prospect for commitment, invokes a sense of urgency, and gets the business relationship in writing.

When prospects have few objections and you have shown you can ultimately satisfy them, your success rate is 64 percent. Instead of defensively responding to your prospect when an objection is raised, use the LARV (Listen, Acknowledge, Respond, and Validate) method to make certain you are taking the time to get to the cause of the roadblock stopping you from finalizing an agreement. Understanding and writing down the different types of objections you received and knowing how to correctly respond to them will result in your fluidity in responding to future objections.

It's surprising how many salespeople don't end up closing deals because they forget to or flat out don't ask for the sale. This is because most people have a fear of rejection, a lack of confidence, or are not educated on how and when is the right time to ask for commitment. You have done all the hard work in comprehending your prospect's needs and wants, along with demonstrating the value of your offering. Your project or service is clearly a valuable solution for this person. You have earned the right to take it one step further and ask for their adherence. With such a variety of closing techniques at your exposure, there's no reason not to confidently ask for the sale.

Invoking urgency, an effective closing technique that will light a fire under your prospect, is essential if you want to get your prospect moving quickly. Instead of having a deal sit around for weeks or months on end, build a sense of urgency by offering incentives, connecting pain points, moving up next step dates, and more. Everyone is on their own timeline with their own list of commitments. Understanding this fact and connecting how your solution will make their lives easier or even better will result in faster commitments by your prospects.

Lastly, your agreement isn't formalized until you have it in writing. Contracts are imperative tools for the salesperson to guarantee prosperity for both parties. Always consult with a lawyer when finalizing your agreement but start off with an outline highlighting the key areas of the business relationship. Whether it's compensation, term of obligations, or safety measures, all of the relevant areas need to be recognized. This is not only to save you if something goes wrong. It also helps get you paid, limits liability, and helps build trust and transparency between you and your new client.

CHAPTER 8
CLOSING THE DEAL—A CASE STUDY

Closing A Deal with Talent

You have the perfect script and a large sum of funding in place and you are ready to find the talented prospects who will be starring in your independent film. Whether it's a top A-List actress with an entourage of agents and managers behind her, or an upcoming novice actor who only has a resume of short films, there is no shortage of talent in the world of independent film. You finally find a talented actor or actress and offer them a deal, thinking they will be fine with whatever you offer them, especially since they've expressed how badly they want the role. Unfortunately, you will quickly realize this is not the case.

You will come across two different types of actors: union and non-union. If your prospective talent is a Screen Actors Guild (SAG) or the Actor's Equity Association and the American Federation of Television and Radio Artists (AFTRA) member, they are protected by a union that specifically looks out for working actors and actresses who are employed on independent and studio projects. They not only set minimum fee requirements for filmed projects, but also extensively control a talent's working conditions, their residuals, travel arrangements, and more. However, if the prospective talent is non-union, meaning they are not associated with any sort of actors union, they don't have any sort of regulations they need to abide by. Keep in mind, although the most recognizable faces in the entertainment industry most likely belong to SAG-AFTRA, in my opinion you are better off hiring non-union actors for your first and second film projects. Not only will hiring non-union talent cost you significantly less, it will also allow you to have a lot more wiggle room for negotiations.

You may think you've found the perfect candidate for the role, but there will always be situations where you will need to "close" this person on the role. Whether it's on compensation, name and likeness, suspension and termination, or health and safety, there are many key areas that need to be discussed with the talent before a deal can be set in place. While it may seem like actors and actresses are willing to get on any project they audition for, this is not the case. They have their own pain points and goals, which the filmmaker must uncover and address in order to convince the talent to play the part. Objections can be raised, resulting in the filmmaker having to effectively answer their concerns and ultimately persuade them to attach themselves to the project. These concerns can be anything from doubts about the character's internal struggle, overlap of commitments that could have an impact on the production shooting schedule, or a strong disagreement on the compensation package offered. The filmmaker must also get the ball moving with talent negotiations and agreements because they are now on a ticking timeline until production starts.

In the following hypothetical case study on the deal closing phase of "Get It in Writing," I will explain the elements needed in an initial talent agreement with a non-repped, non-union actress. At this point in the process the filmmaker has already identified the actress's personal barriers and goals and has demonstrated the value of their project. The filmmaker is now ready to move into the deal closing stage and must finally get a commitment locked down if they want to secure her. Production is right around the corner, and the filmmaker will need to draft a talent agreement outlining their working relationship. As I am not a lawyer, please note the following elements are only personal suggestions to initially outline. However, I highly suggest you also consult with a lawyer for all legal activities pertaining to your film project.

Talent Agreement Goals

A contract is a legally enforceable binding agreement between two or more parties. Contracts are a vital component in building relationships and completing certain business transactions. Without them there is room for misinterpretation and nonadherence to the agreement that may have been initially negotiated between both parties. Agreements have three main goals:

- Serve as an informative and concise record of all commitments between both parties

- Prevent conflicts and mitigate potential risks by holding both parties accountable

- Help you navigate the complexities of the law if you ever find yourself in a legal battle

Talent Agreement Elements

Depending on the scope of your project, your non-union talent agreement will likely have a variety of elements directly related to your talent's participation. Areas include how long this person will be expected to work, how much and how they will receive payment, and their role obligations and what is expected of them. These items are all outlined in this document to make certain both parties understand the extent of the relationship. Keep in mind, since you are dealing with non-union talent, you will *not* have to abide by SAG-AFTRA's requirements. When initially drafting a talent agreement, you want to ask yourself what relevant sections you will want to include to ensure you are thoroughly outlining and communicating what is expected from both you and the talent.

Here are a few major elements one would find in a non-union talent agreement for an independent project:

Engagement Overview

The engagement overview is a high-level summary of what the agreement is for. It establishes a written agreement the parties have made and to fix their rights and duties in accordance with this agreement. In this case, the document serves as a talent agreement on a motion-picture project and a non-union actor or actress. You must also include the date on which the agreement is being made, along with your name and the name of the talent you are extending an offer to. Make sure you get the talent's professional and legal names.

FIGURE 8A   ENGAGEMENT OVERVIEW—EXAMPLE

This Actor Employment Agreement ("PROJECT TITLE") is made effective July 6, 2020, by and between YOUR NAME (hereinafter "Producer") and TALENT'S NAME (hereinafter "Talent"). Producer intends to produce a feature length motion picture based upon the screenplay tentatively entitled PROJECT TITLE (hereinafter "Project").

Role and Obligations

This element of the contract outlines the name of the role the talent is playing in your project, along with the obligations expected of them. For example, if the name of the lead character in your project is Jonathan, you would include the name in the role description. For the definition of responsibilities of your talent, you will want to include directives like listening to the director and other personnel in charge, rendering their services to the best of their ability, and to keep you informed on their whereabouts during production at all times. If your non-union shoot requires your talent to also perform more than the customary duties, you should also include these additional duties in this section. For example, if an actress is also willing to perform makeup services, you should outline this here. This section should spell out what their job is in relation to the project as a whole.

FIGURE 8B   ROLE AND OBLIGATIONS—EXAMPLE

Producer hereby engages Talent to render services as such in the role of "Jonathan" in the motion picture PROJECT TITLE.

Talent agrees:
a. To render your services to the best of your skill and ability in willing collaboration with such persons as we may designate at such times and places as we require;
b. To obtain knowledge of any comply with all rules and regulations for the time being in force at such places where your services are rendered hereunder;
c. To keep us informed of your whereabouts at all times during the period in which your services are required under this agreement;
d. To indemnify us against any and all claims, costs and/or damages made against us as a result of any breach or non-performance by you of any or all of the provisions of this agreement; and
e. To be completely available to enter into and to perform this agreement and have not entered and will not enter into any professional or other commitment that would or might conflict with the full and due rendering of your services hereunder.

Terms and Availability Dates

This area highlights the dates for which your talent must be available to the production company. Although they may be acting only during production and reshoots, talent also needs to be available for rehearsals, wardrobe fittings, and other activities, ensuring a successful performance. This includes everything from pre-production, production, post-production, and additional publicity and promotional pursuits. You will need to define a specific start date from which the talent will begin getting paid for their services.

For pre-production, you need to include the number of days your talent will need to be available for activities like rehearsals, makeup, and wardrobe fittings. You may also want to schedule a script read-through with the entire cast and crew, which will take a few hours out of everyone's calendar. Since these days will most likely not be consecutive, be sure to negotiate with the talent on days that work for them prior to drafting this section of the agreement.

Production is the time period for which the talent must be at hand for shooting. Since production usually takes place within a large time frame, it is typical to list all of the days and weeks that your talent's services will be exclusive to the project. For example, if you are shooting Monday through Friday for the first three weeks of August, you would clearly outline these dates.

Once the production has been completed, talent will need to be available during requested post-production activities, including additional ADR work, reshoots, looping, and more. Unfortunately, you never know how your shoot will go, and oftentimes you may find yourself needing to reshoot certain scenes or acquiring better audio. It is a smart idea to first consult with the talent on what days and weeks after the shoot the actor would be available to perform these duties.

Lastly, it is advised to include the terms of availability for publicity and promotional work along with free days. You may want to shoot some promotional photos for your press kit, website, and film poster, or you may want to get interviews from all of your cast members to share with news outlets. If your film gets into a festival, you may also want your lead actor or actress to make an appearance. If you are shooting your film Monday through Friday during the first three weeks of August, you should include that your talent has Saturdays and Sundays off. Be as specific as possible when it comes to the dates their services will be needed.

FIGURE 8C   TERMS AND AVAILABILITY DATES—EXAMPLE

The term of employment hereunder shall begin on or about July 6, 2020 (the "Start Date") and continue until on or about August 3, 2021 (the "End Date"). The term shall include pre-production, production, post-production, and publicity and promotional activities. Terms of employment is as follows:

Continued

Pre-Production: July 6 through July 9, July 13, and July 22, 2020
Production: August 3 through August 7, August 10 through August 14, August 17 through August 21, 2020
Post-production: October 5 through October 13, 2020
Publicity/Promotion: Producer will reach out to Talent to inquire about availability within at least a five- to seven-day notice period. Talent will not be required for more than five days of publicity and promotion duties.

Compensation, Credit, and Perks

This section includes everything the talent will receive as a result of their services. This includes money, on-screen credit of their name in the film's opening sequence, IMDb credit, an all-expenses-paid hotel room during the production, and more. For compensation on a non-union project, your talent will most likely be paid with fixed compensation unless they have agreed to work for only credit and a copy of the film. Keep in mind, you can always defer compensation to a later date or offer profit participation, in which the talent will get a portion of the producer's adjusted gross. Of course, this would only be attractive if there is already distribution lined up or a good chance the project will be profitable. You usually will set a day rate for every day you will need the talent to perform their services. This can be anywhere from a few dollars to a few hundred dollars.

Credits are also an important form of currency for actors. Having their name on the big screen is a common dream among filmmakers and actors. Ways to negotiate one's credit include their on-screen credit placement at the beginning and end of the film, IMDb credit, and credits on promotional materials like trailers and movie posters. Offering your talent an "associate producer" credit or free headshots can get you a positive reaction while also saving you money.

Perks are fringe benefits not counted as part of the salary. This includes per diem, transportation costs, hotel accommodations, video copies of the film, a dressing room, and more. You will want to be fair with all of the actors on your project and not only provide your lead actress with a luxurious five-star hotel room. Since you are producing a low-budget independent film, you will want to be smart with your money and not throw it all away on hotel accommodations and daily meals of lobster and steak for the cast and crew. However, keep in mind that you should always cover the transportation costs of your talent. They are spending their own money to get to and from locations for your project, and it is only right to compensate them for this type of expense.

FIGURE 8D   COMPENSATION, CREDIT, AND PERKS—EXAMPLE

The salary per working day is $200 USD, with a total of 28 working days. Talent will be paid via check on the last day of production. Talent accepts such engagement upon the terms herein specified. In addition to $200 USD per working day, the following will be paid for by Producer:

- Roundtrip airfare from LAX to Montreal, Canada. First flight leaving August 1, 2020, and return flight of your choice (cannot exceed over a month after shooting is finished)
- Three meals per day (breakfast, lunch, and dinner) during days of shooting. Producer is not responsible for Talent's food on Talent's free days.
- Car service to and from LAX and Montreal's airport
- Airbnb accommodations in a two-bedroom apartment in downtown Montreal, Canada. Accommodations include a private kitchen, bathroom, two bedrooms, and outside patio
- IMDb credit
- Copy of the film AFTER it has been submitted and featured at international and domestic film festivals that have been chosen by the Producer. Talent will be able to use the footage for their personal reel.

Rights Granted

This segment of the contract lays out the specific rights granted to the producer. The producer will need the broadest grant of rights feasible to ensure no potential legal disputes or issues arise in the future. Rights granted can be anything from their ability to use the talent's name and picture, the ability to suspended and terminate the talent at any time, and no obligation from the producer to produce the project.

Name and Likeness

For name and likeness, whether it's letting media interview them, photographing them for behind-the-scenes materials, or having an actress's face shown in a scene of your film, the "name and likeness" clause ensures you will be able to use their name and physical likeness for any reason. These reasons can include issuing publicity, advertising, promotion and exploitation of the film, electronic press kits, and more.

FIGURE 8E   NAME AND LIKENESS—EXAMPLE

Producer shall have the exclusive right to use and license the use of Talent's name, photograph, likeness, and/or voice by any means and in connection with the Project and the advertising, publicizing, exhibition, and/or other exploitation of the Project. Talent grants Producer the right to photograph his or her image and likeness and to record his or her voice, performances, poses, actions, plays, and appearances and to use his or her picture, silhouette, and any other reproductions of his or her physical likeness in connection with the motion picture entitled PROJECT TITLE.

The perpetual right to use, as the Producer may desire, all still and motion pictures and soundtrack recordings and records, which may be made of her or his voice in or in connection with the exhibition, advertising, exploitation, or publicity of PROJECT TITLE.

Suspension and Termination

If you ever have to suspend or terminate a relationship with a non-union actor or actress, it is in your best interest to outline the possible reasons for suspension and/or termination in your talent agreement so that the talent is fully aware of what not to do. Having duty expectations initially written into a contract will ensure you are able to dismiss them if needed. This includes stating that they must perform their outlined job duties and show up on time or else they will be suspended for a period of time or even terminated. Reasons why a talent may be fired from a project include drastically changing their appearance, performing illegal activities, and failure to show up for the shoot. Talent may also be suspended or terminated for reasons outside their control, including force majeure, which is an act of god (lightning, storms, tornados, hurricanes, etc.).

FIGURE 8F   SUSPENSION AND TERMINATION—EXAMPLE

- If we are unable to make use of all or any of your services hereunder for any reason or event beyond our control, we may, by written notice to you, suspend this agreement with immediate effect. If the suspension continues for a period of seven (7) consecutive days or more, we shall be entitled to terminate this agreement with immediate effect.
- If at any time you fail or refuse to perform your services or you breach any and all of the provisions of this agreement, we may, by written or oral notice (but if oral subsequently confirmed in writing), at our discretion either suspend and/or terminate this agreement with immediate effect.
- We shall be entitled to terminate this agreement at any time on giving to you one (1) weeks notice in writing.

No Obligation to Produce

Although you are working in your best interest to produce a film project, if in the case you don't successfully complete the project, it should not be held against you. By also establishing the producer's right of no obligation to produce, they are protecting themselves from any form of contention with the talent. This is because the talent may feel like they wasted their time or have expected a desired result that may or may not come to fruition.

FIGURE 8G   NO OBLIGATION TO PRODUCE—EXAMPLE

While producer shall use his/her best efforts to effect a production hereunder, nothing herein shall be construed to obligate Producer to produce, distribute, release, perform, or exhibit a film based upon the Work, in whole or in part, or otherwise to exercise, exploit or make any use of the rights, license, privileges, or property gained herein to Producer.

Health and Safety

This section states that you will do everything in your best efforts to ensure health, safety, and welfare of the talent during the project. However, if you are not offering personal insurance to your talent during production and something does happen to them, you won't be held liable and will not be responsible for any medical bills related to their accident. In this section you also want to ensure your talent has no pre-existing health issues you are not aware of that might impact their ability to fulfill their obligations.

FIGURE 8H   HEALTH AND SAFETY—EXAMPLE

Talent has no health conditions that would undermine their ability to perform their duties outlined in this agreement. Producer will use his/her best efforts to ensure Talent's health, safety, and welfare during the project. There will be no stunts that will require a gun handler, stunt performer, animal handler, etc. Talent is responsible for making smart and safe decisions while shooting on set. Producer is not responsible for the medical bill for the result of injury caused by Talent's physical or emotional actions.

Talent acknowledges the Talent's obligation to obtain appropriate insurance coverage for the benefit of the Talent. Producer is not responsible for insurance coverage for Talent.

Exhibition of Project and Confidentiality

Since your actors and crew have access to the screenplay, daily footage, and other valuable items, it's in your best interest to make sure they stay under wraps. It's important to provide a statement outlining how your actor or crew member cannot divulge or disclose anything related to the confidential information.

FIGURE 8I   EXHIBITION OF PROJECT AND CONFIDENTIALITY—EXAMPLE

Talent may have access to proprietary, private and/or confidential information ("Confidential Information") of Producer and Project. Confidential

---

Continued

Information shall mean all non-public information, which constitutes, relates or refers to the operation of the Project, including, without limitations, all financial investment, operational, personnel, sales, marketing, statistical information of the Project.

Talent will not at any time or in any manner, either directly or indirectly, use for the personal benefit of Talent, or divulge, disclose, or communicate in any manner any Confidential Information. Talent will protect such information and treat the Confidential Information as strictly confidential. This provision shall continue to be effective after the termination of this Agreement.

Project's Union Status

To ensure you are not going against any of SAG-AFTRA's requirements, you will want to include a section stating your project's non-union status. Sometimes actors may be untruthful about their union status due to not receiving an adequate amount of work. You want to protect yourself from any possible legal issues surrounding any actors union rules and regulations. In the case when a project is compliant with SAG-AFTRA, a non-union actor may receive the ability to join SAG through a Taft-Hartley agreement. However, since your project is not associated with a union, this will not be the case.

FIGURE 8J   PROJECT'S UNION STATUS—EXAMPLE

Talent has agreed and confirmed that they are NON-UNION status and does not belong to any unions, such as the Screen Actors Guild (SAG) and the American Federation of Television and Radio Artists (AFTRA). This Project is in no way a vehicle to a Taft-Hartley agreement, and introduction to SAG-eligible or SAG status should not be anticipated after the Project's completion.

Contact Information

Last but not least, contact information is an important section to add to your contract because it allows you to know where to send their paycheck to or, more important, how to get a hold of them. Usually a telephone number, email address, and current physical address are sufficient. You will want to confirm that the talent will maintain constant communication with you on scheduling conflicts or any sort of potential impediments to their performance.

FIGURE 8K   CONTACT INFORMATION—EXAMPLE

All notices that the Producer is required to or may desire to give to the Talent may be given either by email or phone call. The correct contact information for Talent is the following:
- Telephone: 888-888-8888
- Email: example@gmail.com
- Address: 123 Filmmaking Lane, Beverly Hills, CA 90210

The Talent must keep the Producer advised as to where the Talent may be reached by telephone without unreasonable delay. Talent is responsible for keeping in contact with the Producer during production. This means not disappearing or being nowhere to be found during a scheduled shoot. Talent will immediately communicate with the Producer on any scheduling conflicts or potential impediments to their performance.

Case Study—A Final Word on Closing the Deal

The above are only a few of the recommended elements to include in a non-union talent agreement. Other general legal sections include arbitration, governing law, assignment, and scope and jurisdiction of the agreement. As mentioned in the previous chapter, you can use the internet, books, and other resources to find pre-made non-union talent agreements. This will provide you with a starting point to ensure you are successful in articulating the breadth of your working relationship with the talent.

When dealing with non-union talent, remember to only cast actors and actresses who display enthusiasm for their craft and, more important, your project. It's also imperative to ensure you get along with this person on a personal level since you will be working with them for a long period of time. Also, you want someone who has worked on an indie project before and is fully aware of the grassroots and guerilla style of filmmaking. Nobody enjoys having a prima donna on set who kills the project's collaborative spirit. You can find non-union actors in a variety of ways, including casting websites like LACasting.com, Backstage, and even Craigslist. If you have the budget, engage a casting agent to help you in the casting process. They will have an educated sense of what to look for in connection to the role you are casting for and the project as a whole.

Closing the deal happens in many forms. Overcoming objections and asking for commitment is one thing, but it's a whole other level to establish your agreement in writing and have both parties sign off on it. Written agreements make it official and oftentimes are needed to land a distributor, since they will require what is known as a "chain of title." This document includes all of the written agreements between your talent, crew members, location owners, and more. Without these signed agreements in place, a distributor will not be able to exhibit your film due to the risk of getting sued. It's also crucial that you have your contracts finalized and signed at the beginning in the pre-production stage instead of trying to get them signed after the film has been shot and you've received an offer for distribution. What if your talent decides to hold your project hostage by demanding a higher amount of compensation in return? In this case you have spent all your time and money on a project that will never see the light of day. Whether you are dealing with a writer, distributor, actor, financier, or crew member, get your agreement in writing!

STAGE V

RELATIONSHIP SUCCESS

CHAPTER 9
RELATIONSHIP SUCCESS

Defining Relationship Success

Congratulations! You have successfully closed a deal and formed a new business relationship. You went from humble beginnings of researching your prospect and learning about their wants and needs to demonstrating the value of your project or service, addressing every objection, and getting agreement from your prospect and ultimately confirming it in writing. Does this mean the sales cycle stops here? Absolutely not.

Most people think the sales process ends after closing the deal, which explains why a lot of salespeople eventually fail at meeting their customer's expectations. There is one more stage most people aren't aware of. Relationship success is the fifth and final stage of the sales process, and it concentrates on keeping your clients and business partners happy. It consists of anticipating their challenges, questions, and needs, and providing solutions and answers to those issues.

In relationship success a salesperson is focused on working proactively with their clients to assist them in getting more value out of their purchase. Improving the happiness and loyalty of your clients will help protect your bottom line by reducing the churn rate and improving satisfaction. Relationship success ultimately keeps the business partnership alive and well for both the salesperson and the client.

Relationship Success Goals

Relationship success is a commonly overlooked stage in the sales process to make certain you are:

- Keeping your client actively in the loop on relevant developments and updates

- Resolving conflicts that may arise at any point during the relationship

- Using a positive attitude to exceed client expectations and garner upsell opportunities

Relationship Success Steps

There are four main steps in the relationship success process: providing an onboarding session and periodic check-ins, resolving conflicts, using a positive attitude through a variety of techniques, and, lastly, developing and upselling your clients.

Step #1: Provide Onboarding and Updates

Have you ever purchased a product and had no idea how to use it? Have you ever bought a service and had no clue on where to start it? Once the salesperson sold it to you, did they drift off into the abyss and leave you standing there to figure it out all on your own? No one likes to feel lost and alone, especially on something they have excitedly agreed to partake in.

This is where onboarding and updates come into play. Providing some sort of initial onboarding session will make your client extremely happy and satisfied to know they are being supported throughout the entire process of working with you. In addition, your client will also appreciate periodic updates highlighting any sort of progress on the project or service you offered them. Whether it's sharing important and relevant updates via emails, phone calls, or other communication methods, or introducing your new client to your team and vice versa, it will guarantee an uncomplicated and prosperous business relationship. As a freelance independent film-maker, whether you are a cinematographer, color specialist, or editor, once you close a deal with a client you will need to brief them on your process. Delivering pieces of work to the client and working within a timeline, the freelance independent filmmaker must make sure they have their ducks in a row in order to successfully deliver a product or service the client will be happy with. Likewise, a producer will most likely have to provide investors with a monthly (or even weekly) status update on the project they invested hundreds of thousands of dollars in. They will also have to walk through a newly employed crew member on the logistics of the project and the expectations surrounding the role the crew member is filling.

The Onboarding Process

When most people are hired for a new job, on the first day they participate in what is called an onboarding meeting. The goal of this meeting is to introduce the new employee to major areas, including the breakdown of the company's team members, the company's internal processes, role expectations, and more. Sales-people do the same, but for their clients. A salesperson would introduce the new client to relevant team members of theirs the client will be working with, along with being introduced to the relevant team members on the client's side. The onboarding meet-ing is reserved to cover major deliverables and responsibilities, including a timeline of action.

As an independent filmmaker, once you are hired on a gig, you will be expected to deliver on what you have pitched to your client in the beginning of the sales process. Likewise, if you are a film producer who hired a crew member, you will need to kick things off to make certain he or she is fully aware of the project's logistics. Here is a five-step guide on how to conduct an onboarding meeting:

1. **Send a Welcome Email:** At this point the contract has already been signed and the payment negotiations have been worked out between both parties. To get the relationship started on the right foot, send an email highlighting how excited you are to get started working with your new client or crew member. Let them know your goal is to support them every step of the way and that you view this relationship as a partnership. At the end of your email include a call-to-action of scheduling an onboarding session, with the goal to introduce important team members and to cover all deliverables and processes. You should always aim to schedule an in-person meeting, as it will help build a bond among all team members involved. Independent film producers can send welcome emails to key creative heads or even financiers, as much as freelance editors or cinematographers can send welcome emails to the filmmaker who hired them on the project.

2. **Pick Your Team and Hold an Internal Meeting:** Based on the available resources, and if it makes sense, choose the appropriate people to take on your new client. If you are an editor and you happen to have additional team members behind you whom you can use on a specific project, like an assistant editor or someone who focuses solely on special effects, you should include them in the process. If you are a producer who secured financing from an investor, having other important producers from the project be in the loop will make your life a whole lot easier. If a producer hired a head of a creative department, he or she will want to include the other heads. Once you have your team assembled, hold an internal meeting covering who the client or crew member is, what goals and expectations you have laid out, and any other relevant information that will help your team in servicing your new client in the best way possible.

3. **Schedule an Onboarding Meeting:** Like you did for the discovery call in stage two, you want to come prepared to this meeting

with a series of questions and objectives for promoting the overall success of your working relationship with your client. With a bullet-proof call agenda, you will aim to define expectations and set milestones for the project or service you have promised them. Gather any sort of helpful data or information in getting the job done. This can be anything from a cinematographer getting the lowdown on the director's vision to a producer briefing a creative head on what he or she needs to accomplish by set dates. The onboarding meeting is a time when your team and their team can connect and make certain everyone is on the same page. The act of having an onboarding meeting in the first place demonstrates how much you value communication and transparency. Be sure to also utilize collaborative technology tools like Google Docs to efficiently keep track of everything. Most importantly, having an onboarding meeting establishes that you have a set plan of action to achieve the objectives you have outlined previously in the deal closing stage.

4. **Follow up:** Around twenty-four hours after the onboarding meeting, be sure to send a follow-up email with everyone cc'd who participated. Thank everyone for their time and reiterate how excited you are to get things rolling. In your follow-up email, briefly highlight the topics explored during the meeting. This can be done with a simple bullet-point list or it can link the entire team to a shared Google Doc or spreadsheet. Most importantly, also include a timeline breakdown of deliverables and workflows. For example, an editor would request a client send a hard drive of the raw footage of the film. A producer would first send example image styles to a graphic designer before the graphic designer can start their endeavors.

5. **Do a Check-up Call:** Lastly, remember to always keep in touch with your client. Don't leave them hanging after you have finished onboarding them. You should always follow up with your client periodically to identify if they have any additional questions or concerns. When an independent film producer receives funding from an investor, he or she should send weekly updates on how

everything is progressing during the film shoot, along with post-production. An investor will deeply appreciate receiving exciting images and footage from all the action happening on set. The same goes with a creative head or producer checking in on a crew member during production. Only check in with clients if you have some sort of value to add. This can be anything from additional information or updates on your project's or service's progress, a resolution to a problem they have expressed, or some other exciting opportunity they may be interested in.

Step #2: Resolve Conflicts

Every healthy relationship consists of some form of conflict. Two people can't expect to agree with one another on everything all the time. Most people are afraid of conflict and respond by quickly running away from it. However, the key is not to avoid conflict but to address it head on by resolving it in a healthy manner. Resolving conflicts is a major part of relationship success because when conflict isn't handled properly, it can cause a great deal of harm to the relationship, thus also resulting in failed business projects. It's simply not good for business.

There are many ways conflicts can occur between two individuals. Mostly conflicts flare up due to differences in values, motivations, perceptions, ideas, or desires. Even though a conflict might appear to be trivial to one person, it can trigger strong emotional feelings and a deep personal need by the other individual involved. The needs of each party play a crucial role in the long-term success of a relationship. It goes without saying that both parties deserve respect and consideration. A lack of communication and understanding about differing needs can end up in both parties distancing themselves, arguing with each other, and negatively impacting the dynamic of the entire team. Having a sense of emotional awareness will make it easier for you to understand where others are coming from. You won't be able to effectively communicate or resolve disagreements if you can't identify how or why *you* feel a certain way.

Since independent filmmaking is a collaborative activity, there is no doubt conflicts will come up at some point. Some of these conflicts can include arguments between a director and an actress on the correct vision of her character, disagreements on a long shooting schedule, lack of communication to the props and wardrobe department, and more. When conflicts occur during production, it can potentially be extremely troublesome. Given how much money and time is at stake, fires need to be put out as quickly as possible to ensure the production continues to run smoothly.

Here are some helpful tips to keep in mind when resolving conflicts on and off a film set:

- **Accept Conflict:** The first step is to accept that conflict will occur at some point in the process. Since conflict is unavoidable, we must be open to learning how to manage it. Many times conflicts are opportunities for growth and improved communication. When it comes down to managing the crew members on your project or managing the expectations of the client you are freelancing for, accept that conflict is part of the deal.

- **Analyze the Conflict:** Taking a step back and analyzing what is happening will help in assessing the best mode of action to solve the conflict. Some questions you might want to ask yourself can revolve around what specifically triggered the conflict, whether the conflict is accurate or exaggerated, what parties are involved, and some initial ideas on how to potentially solve the conflict. Since these are invested emotions and feelings, it's not a good idea to jump right in with solutions without fully analyzing the core issues at hand.

- **Establish the Leader Early On:** You want to make sure the command structure is not fragmented or weak in any way, or you will end up fighting more because everyone will be vying for control. Having people on set constantly questioning your authority and slowing down progress is of no use to anyone's time. Whether it's your director who is in charge of everyone on set, or certain creative heads who manage crew members in their department, you must draw out a food chain outlining the power ranking of each individual involved.

- **Avoid Personal Attacks:** As much as there is an outstanding conflict impacting everyone involved, the last thing you want to do is insult the other party. People don't typically agree with someone who insults them, and because the goal is to resolve the conflict, insulting them is not a viable option. Insulting also includes belittling them, using sarcasm, rolling your eyes, and more. If you want to get this person to quickly agree with you and move on, both of you will need to respect each other. Since respect is earned, throwing a jab at them will cost you everything.

- **Decide What Results You Want:** There is no effective way of resolving a conflict if you don't have an idea of what you want to accomplish. You need to ask yourself if you are trying to change someone's beliefs. Are you defending the actions of yourself or someone else? Would getting rid of this person solve the problem, or is it a systemic problem? If you don't have a clear vision of the outcome you want, there's no reason to be involving yourself in the conflict in the first place. It might be best if you decided to drop the issue instead of pursuing it.

- **Preparation Meetings:** In the case where team members may feel blindsided by a decision on a project, it's best to commence a series of preparation meetings to make certain everyone is on the same page. Examples of being blindsided on set include an actress disliking a change in her wardrobe, a cinematographer who doesn't agree with a director's visual approach to an important scene in the film, or an editor who doesn't understand why he or she is being asked to delete the first half of their second cut. Holding rehearsals for the actors and preparation meetings (including all departments and their respective crew members) will ensure everyone is constantly communicating with each other on updates, deletions, changes, and more. These meetings can be held once or twice a week, depending on the circumstances.

- **Be Willing to Compromise:** It's not worth anyone's time to go back and forth over who's right and who's wrong. The truth of the matter is: there wouldn't be a conflict in the first place if both parties didn't believe they were correct. Oftentimes people will argue for the sake of argument and have the goal of not backing down until they "win." However, conflicts don't necessarily have to have a loser. Be the bigger person and meet the other person halfway. By deciding what's most important to you, swallowing your pride, and slightly surrendering your stance, you are setting a stage where both parties have a chance to win.

- **Focus on the Future and Share Interests:** Instead of wasting your energy dwelling over all the things bothering you about the person, including past scenarios where they were a problem, you should instead focus on the future with this person. Take ownership of the problem and recognize that no matter how the past came about, you need to develop a strategy to address the present conflict and the potential conflicts that may arise in the future. The future of your working relationship and the project are at stake. Emphasizing the future goals and how badly both of you want to achieve them will help shine a light on solving the conflict. Sharing your interests will provide the other person with a better understanding of why you have a particular stance. Take the time to question the other party on their interests and attempt to identify any common ground.

Step #3: Positive Attitude

A positive attitude won't only help you in your relationships, it will also help you lead a happy life and help you conquer your desired level of professional success. When you practice positivity, dealing with professional or personal roadblocks will be a lot easier, and you will be able to power through in the face of adversity. A positive attitude has a variety of health benefits, including an increased life span, lower rate of depression, and better coping skills during hard times.

In relationship success, having a positive attitude will allow you to successfully address any potential conflicts while also encouraging a spirit of cooperation and collaboration.

How does one implement a positive attitude even during stressful times? It starts with self-talk. Self-talk is your internal unspoken thoughts that run through your head. These thoughts are either positive or negative, and they develop through logic and reason. If all of the thoughts running through your head are mainly negative, your outlook on life is more likely to be pessimistic. On the other hand, if your thoughts are mainly positive, you have an optimistic outlook. Someone who has more positive thoughts tends to consistently practice positive thinking. For example, if a producer is constantly complaining about how they can't get any investors to see the value of their project, don't you think it has an impact on their motivation? Their defeatist attitude will be easy to read by other potential investors.

No one wants to work with a grouch, especially in such a fun and collaborative pursuit like independent filmmaking. How you present yourself and your attitude toward situations, whether it's on a phone call, in a production meeting, or even on a film set, plays a huge role in how others perceive you. Constantly complaining, taking ideas personally, or hanging around negative people will provide no value to yourself and the people around you. People complain because they automatically anticipate the worst and see things in a polarizing way, either good or bad. However, there's an entire grey area they overlook. On the contrary, practicing positive self-talk, asking yourself what you are thinking, and being open to laugh at adversity will put you in a better state of mind, which will positively resonate with others. Individuals who adopt a positive attitude see the good in everything and fully comprehend that things aren't either black or white.

Here are some ways you can adopt a positive attitude on a daily basis:

- **Live a Healthy Life:** It's very difficult to remain positive when your body and your mind are consumed with rubbish. This rubbish includes eating boxes of chocolate cookies, watching heartbreaking television news stories, and consuming a sea of whiskey. Instead, think of your body as a temple. Aim to exercise at least thirty minutes a day. Whether it's going on a run, lifting weights, or playing a sport, exercise will dramatically and positively affect your mood and reduce stress levels. In addition, you should follow a healthy diet to provide fuel to your mind and your body. It's extremely hard to do your job when you have the negative baggage of poor eating and exercise habits standing in the way.

- **Surround Yourself With Positive People:** You don't need to understand rocket science to know that surrounding yourself with negative people will result in you becoming a negative person. Negative individuals will increase your stress levels and make you doubt your ability in all areas of your life. Questioning and judging you on your thoughts and actions, complaining about the elements holding them back in life, being fearful to chase their dreams, and sucking all the energy out of you are all signs someone is a negative influence. How do you expect to be able to conquer the world when you are surrounded by people who criticize you and hold you back? Instead, surround yourself with likeminded individuals who share the same passion, energy, and enthusiasm in everything they do. This especially applies to independent film crews, since you will be spending a significant amount of time with this group of people. One bad apple can negatively impact the dynamics of the project's team.

- **Practice Positive Self-Talk:** Take the golden rule of "treat others as you want to be treated" and also apply this to yourself. Refrain from saying anything to yourself you wouldn't say to someone else. Be kind and encouraging with yourself and recognize you are trying your best. If a negative idea pops in your head, instead of dwelling on the idea, rationally evaluate it instead. Think hard about why this thought materialized in the first place and respond with affirmations that include good things about yourself. Whether it's how great the film project is going, the amount of clients you have pleased in the past with your freelance editing services, or the recognition you have received at prior film festivals, focus your energy and attention on these types of thoughts instead. Fully embracing positive self-talk will surely take some time and practice, but it's important to get started as soon as possible.

- **Be Aware of the Good Things:** It's easy to fall into a trap of pessimism if everything on your mind is focused on negative events and obstacles standing in your way. Independent film-makers naturally deal with negative events all the time. Production running behind schedule, projects going over budget, or distributors turning down their films are a few examples of how negativity can make way its way into the filmmaking process. However, instead of investing your time and energy in focusing on the negatives, shift your focus on the positive. Most individuals have a lot more to be thankful for than they realize. For example, if a distribution company turns your film down, instead think about all the potential opportunities this has provided. This means you can submit your film to other prospective distributors and eventually find a good fit. It means this particular distributor wasn't the one meant for your project.

- **Practice Dealing With Rejection:** Salespeople deal with rejection every single day. Handling rejection correctly is a skillset you can develop, and once you do, you will have a smoother time remaining positive. Put yourself out there and don't be afraid to request things that may or may not work out. Asking the girl out, asking for a promotion, or submitting your film to Sundance and Cannes are all ways one can practice dealing with rejection. Once you have encountered several rejections, being told no will be less scary than before. Commit to one week of putting yourself out there and not holding back from asking others for things you may or may not receive. Be comfortable with the word *no*. A no will bring you closer to a yes because you identify some sort of objection holding the other individual back. We don't know what the future holds, and you have nothing to lose by asking, so you might as well ask for what you want.

- **Laugh At Yourself:** You learned about the importance of comedy in building rapport and telling personal stories to demonstrate value. Using comedy and being able to laugh also comes in handy when it comes to positive thinking. By giving yourself permission to smile and laugh, especially during troubling times, it will make hardships feel easier to endure. Confronting your fear of being ridiculed and asking yourself what's the worst thing that can happen are ways you can take the negative circumstance and identify ways to laugh at it. The negative circumstances you may experience do not define who you are as a person. Laughing decreases stress and positively impacts your physical and mental health in many other ways. Remember, we are all human and we are not perfect. If you can't laugh at the issue while it's happening, tell yourself how you look forward to looking back and laughing at this point of time in your life.

Step #4: Develop and Upsell

In every other area of your life, you should always be aiming to grow, which also includes the relationship you have with your client. This is because developing and upselling in your relationships has the power to assist in growing your base of advocates and promoters. Upselling is when you sell a more expensive version of a product or service to a current client, along with selling them on additional project or service opportunities. For example, a filmmaker can upsell a client by proposing an additional five videos with a 30 percent discount. Establishing your best intentions to realize your client's success will result in more happy and loyal relationships, referrals for more business, and an increase in revenue opportunities. If you have proven to be an efficient video content creator for a client, they will gladly continue working with you and even refer their personal network to you. Likewise, if you demonstrate an ability to empower your crew members, they will want to work with you again in the future.

Here are a five ways you can effectively develop and upsell your clients, independent contractors, employees, and other business relationships:

- **Ask for Feedback:** Ask a current or past client or employee for feedback regarding the strengths and weaknesses of working with you. Whether it's centered on a film project or a type of service you offered them, it's important to gain some insight into how others feel about the experience. A producer or director can check in with an actress or a crew member about their experience working on set, or a freelance video content creator can check in with their client to see how everything is going. Clients, independent contractors, and employees will deeply appreciate you touching base with them, as it demonstrates you care about them. While you are at it, if they express their experience has been positive, they can even write a testimonial for you.

- **Reward Loyalty:** You are fully aware of the hard work it takes to identify a prospect and turn them into a client. It also takes a lot of work to find an all-star core film crew. Instead of finding new leads, reward your clients and encourage repeat business by offering incentives like special deals, early access, discounts, etc. If you're a freelance filmmaker working on video projects for a client, see if you can work out a multiproject deal using perks. Also think about applying a referral incentive program, which would bring more business your way. A way to incentivize your crew members if you're a filmmaker working on a project is to praise the work they have been doing and to insist you will continue to work with them on future projects.

- **Treat Clients and Your Team Like People, Not Like Business:** Instead of thinking of your client or crew member as little more than a paycheck, you should think of them as a person like yourself. Take an interest in their personal life. If you know they are a parent, ask them about how their children are doing. If you find out they are interested in reading books, recommend a few of your favorite books to them. When in conversation, ask questions about their interests, hobbies, values, etc. Because people love talking about themselves, let them do all the talking. They will walk away from the conversation thinking about how rare it is to find someone who genuinely cares.

■ **Give Them Access to Your Network:** If you discover in a conversation with your client that they are looking for help in a certain area, take inventory of who is in your personal network. Assess if there is anyone you know who would be able to help them in the identified area of interest. Whether they need a new lawyer, accountant, plumber, or music composer, refer them to someone who you believe would be able to help them out. You not only will be assisting this person, you will also be doing a service to the person you are referring them to. Who knows, this person might do the same for you one day.

■ **Exceed Expectations:** One of the most effective ways to build a strong relationship with a client is to develop a reputation as someone who delivers exceptional service and results. You never want to overpromise and oversell yourself and your offering, because it might come back and bite you in the end if things don't work as planned. Instead, it's better to provide a realistic proposal with reasonable expectations you can easily deliver. This way, when the project or service is completed, you will impress the client with the final project. As a freelance filmmaker, this can be anything from delivering the project in an aesthetically pleasing format, hand-delivering the materials, and walking them through everything in person. Going beyond your client's expectations will make them want to work with you again and refer you to everyone they know.

Relationship Success Summary

Whether you are a producer trying to keep their investor happy, a director attempting to keep their crew at bay, or a freelance video content creator trying to put a smile on your client's face, independent filmmakers from all walks of life must understand the significance of relationship success. As the fifth and final stage of the sales process, relationship success is where the sale truly begins, which is something most salespeople aren't aware of. The general consensus is: once you close a deal, all the work is completed, so you can sit back and relax. However, this isn't the case. Even after a deal has been closed, you are constantly selling on a daily basis by developing and upselling your independent contractors, employees, clients, and business partners. The same holds true if you are an independent filmmaker. Whether you are a producer, director, or other key creative head who's developing a relationship with a cast and crew, or you're a freelancer who's fostering a relationship with a client, the relationship doesn't end at the close. Providing an onboarding session and periodic check-ins, resolving conflicts, cultivating a positive attitude, and developing and upselling your clients are all significant ways to express your desire for the relationship to succeed.

The first step of relationship success consists of holding an onboarding meeting. This meeting will ensure that everyone is on the same page and that no one is left in the dark. Taking the time to wrangle up the appropriate team members, establish a timeline of deliverables, and build even more rapport will take your relationship to the next level. Onboarding meetings result in increased efficiency, chances of more clients and upsell opportunities, and an overall happier business relationship. As a filmmaker, you want to set your crew members and cast up for success, along with the work you will be doing for a client. Onboarding meetings provide an opportunity to answer any outstanding questions, clarify role descriptions, and set the overall tone for the partnership.

Solving conflicts when they arise and having a positive attitude every step of the way also enable relationship success. Conflict is a discernible element apparent in every relationship. Instead of running away from conflict, you must learn to embrace it and actively choose to solve it. Conflicts take place due to differences in values, motivations, perceptions, ideas, or desires. They happen on phone calls, in-person meetings, and even on film sets. Analyzing the conflict, refraining from personal attacks, focusing on the future, and sharing common goals are all ways you can go about working out your differences. When it comes to adopting a positive attitude, one must initially investigate his or her internal self-talk and ask: *Am I being negative or self-critical?* Surrounding yourself with positive likeminded individuals, practicing the experience of being rejected, and laughing at yourself and the situation at hand are ways to look on the bright side.

Lastly, relationship success is all about fostering relationships and setting yourself up for additional opportunities. Developing and upselling your clients are ways to exemplify your desire to see your client succeed. Asking for feedback, offering loyalty incentives, and exceeding your client's expectations are a few ways you can develop and upsell for more opportunities. A freelance filmmaker may find it hard enough to identify the right opportunity for their services. Through developing their current and past clients, the filmmaker will, in turn, earn more referrals, which will turn into more clients and more money, allowing them to continue doing what they love.

CHAPTER 10
RELATIONSHIP SUCCESS— A CASE STUDY

Relationship Success with Crew Members

Since filmmaking is a collaborative pursuit consisting of more than one person, you will need to manage relationships with a variety of people through every stage of the filmmaking process. This includes Above the Line individuals (like the cast, screenwriter, producer, and director) along with Below the Line individuals (which includes everyone else—casting directors, cinematographers, gaffers, grips, production assistants, location scouts, and script supervisors). Whether it's dealing with a location scout in pre-production, a gaffer during a shoot, an editor in post-production, or a distributor when the film is ready to be shown to the world, knowing how to manage relationships and solve conflicts will be essential in the overall success of your project.

While producing your independent film project, you will find all sorts of Above the Line and Below the Line individuals who contribute to every aspect of the production. Depending on your budget and the scope of your project, you might find yourself with a skeleton crew compared with a larger crew found on a Hollywood studio film. Most of the time during independent ultra-low-budget productions, people will perform more than one role. For example, a cinematographer might also deal with lighting and electric duties instead of having an additional gaffer and grip on hand.

Despite how large your crew is, whether it's five people or fifty, you will need to be able to lead and put out fires as they occur. Conflicts occur in all sizes, from a small verbal disagreement with one other person to a full-on battle with the entire crew and cast. Anything from failing to delegate key personnel, to enabling unprofessional cast and crew members who undermine your authority, to failing to anticipate schedule changes and equipment needs—all are instances in which a film project can turn into a complete disaster. Although there is no magic formula on how to prevent problems from occurring in the first place, there are a few solutions available to help you deal with these issues when they pop up.

How does a filmmaker correctly solve on-set issues? What specific methods can a filmmaker use to regain control and work out differences? This hypothetical case study will explore the resolving conflict phase of relationship success. I will provide five common conflicts relating to crew members on a project and what you can do to ensure these conflicts do not occur. At this point in the process, you have closed the deal with everyone—from the financiers, crew members, and the talent. The project has been greenlit and they have started shooting their first feature film. However, during production, a few disputes begin to surface and you must effectively solve them in order to maintain order and save the project from looming disaster.

Conflict #1

The Director of Photography with Fancy Equipment but a Lack of Skills

The Conflict

After talking with many potential directors of photography for your project, you think you found the perfect person for the job. They have all the top-notch equipment and are even willing to let you use it for little or no cost. Their equipment consists of a state-of-the-art 8K RED camera, a camera stabilizer mount, and one of the newest aerial drone quadcopters. For an independent filmmaker on a tight budget like yourself, it is a very alluring offer that would make sense to pursue given your desire to increase the production value of your project. The first day of shooting comes around and you quickly realize, despite your director of photography having all this fancy equipment, that they have no idea what they are doing. The shot list is out of whack, there is constant miscommunication between them and the director, and you are way over schedule due to them not being able to set up their shots in a timely manner. Unfortunately, you realize you have made the mistake of hiring someone solely based on the resources they have access to, rather than also accounting for their skills and abilities.

The Solution

Backtracking to the hiring process of your project's director of photography, it's imperative to carefully consider a variety of other factors before you offer the job to anyone based on the equipment they have available. In the prospecting phase, you should have done your initial research on this person. This research consists of identifying every past project they have worked on along with checking out their professional reel. While analyzing their reel, ask yourself if their style and approach is the right look for your project. Even if you think it's a perfect match, you should hold a discovery call and ask questions confirming that their sensibilities align with the direction you have in mind for your film. Directly talking with them and asking them specific questions about the intended aesthetic of your project will do a better job confirming they are the right choice than only looking at what they have done in the past.

You should also plan to do reference checks to feel out whether they will be able to get along with everyone and complement your project's timeline. Reach out to a minimum of two filmmakers the director of photography has worked with in the past. Ask them questions about the prospective director of photography's expertise and ability to get the job done. Relying on one person might not give you the entire picture of what it's like to work with them. If the references check out to your liking, you should plan to have the prospective director of photography meet with your director in person. Since they will be closely working with each other, they must personally get along and share a similar vision. This meeting will allow both parties to get to know each other and recognize if it is an ideal relationship fit.

In the case where you have already started shooting and have realized your director of photography is not a good fit, it may be troubling to accomplish, but you must quickly find a replacement. You have planned and spent way too much time and money for the shoot to go terribly. If everyone on set, including the talent, loses faith in your director of photography's ability to successfully capture the performance, it will inevitably shatter everyone's enthusiasm for the project, thus resulting in bad performances from your talent and hopeless attitudes from the rest of the crew. Through your prospecting pursuits, always have one or two backup choices you would be able to call upon. However, by ensuring you have thoroughly done your due diligence, you should never have to be in this position.

Conflict #2

The Location Scout Who Didn't Account for All the Outside Noise

The Conflict

Your script has a variety of scenes with cool and unique locations and you know the perfect places to shoot all of them—whether it's your brother's apartment located downtown or your friend's massive restaurant in town square. Thinking about what locations you already have available to you, the location scout you hired either doesn't perform a thorough inspection during your location and tech scout before the shoot, or you don't even bother doing them in the first place. Either way, the day of your shoot arrives and you realize there are no places to plug in some of the lighting equipment, nor is there a working bathroom available within ten miles. On top of this, your sound recorder is pointing out that the constant traffic noise outside is being captured on the sound footage, flooding out the actor's voice. Anything from the constant noise of airplanes traveling above you, to a lack of cell phone service to get in touch with someone in case of an emergency, to faulty building construction resulting in injuries—are all potential problems for an uncleared location. Everything is turning out to be a complete disaster on set and you wished you would have done more pre-planning.

The Solution

You should never shoot your project at a location without performing both an initial location and tech scout. For the initial location scout all you need is yourself, your director, and your location scout to join. When performing a location scout, you must ask yourself if the location looks the part and, more important, how it will look on camera. Confirm the location will allow for the type of camera work you are envisioning or that you can move things around to look a certain way. Most importantly, you want to make sure your location is controllable. Are you able to close down the entire restaurant? Are you able to shoot at a time when there will be limited street noises? You also want to guarantee your location provides the necessary resources you and your film crew will need. For example, a working bathroom, adequate room for each department to house their equipment, including makeup and electrical equipment. Also pay attention to the parking situation. Does your crew and cast need to park a few blocks away, or are they able to easily park their cars directly in front of the location? Lastly, you want to make sure the location owner is comfortable with the shooting arrangements. Be transparent with them and don't underestimate the size of your crew or the nature of the shoot. Film shoots are huge disruptions, and your location owner is aware of this. Be honest, get their approval in writing, and overprepare your location.

Once you have identified a location satisfying the initial requirements for your project, you will want to perform another scout devoted to a more comprehensive technical examination, which is done by a variety of key crew members, including the director of photography, production designer, art director, first assistant director, gaffer, key grip, and sound mixer. Each member will inspect everything in relation to their department and duties, including the location's sound, available power outlets, and natural lighting sources. Make sure you include as many key personnel in your tech scout as possible to guarantee they can perform their duties efficiently; this allows you to change the location choice before the shoot, if needed. Since your director of photography and director are on location together, insist they carefully walk through and visualize shots. The more every shot is discussed and planned, the easier the shoot will go.

When choosing the right locations for your project, you must be in constant communication with others on your team. Spending an entire day driving around and checking out various locations can be tiresome, but it's crucial you take the time to discuss each location in detail with your team. You will be in a better position if you need to change shooting locations in pre-production as opposed to being stuck with a location in production and having to deal with it, as too much time, money, and energy has been exerted.

Conflict #3

The Script Supervisor That Never Was

The Conflict

You recently finished a long and laborious four-week shoot. After taking a nap for two weeks, you are finally excited to get started on post-production editing. Your editor begins assembling a first cut and quickly comes to you with some disheartening news. It appears there are a bunch of continuity errors in various shots, negatively impacting the viewing experience. In one shot, your lead actor is holding a pistol in his right hand and in another shot it's in his left hand. You also notice a major difference in the color of your actress's sweater. You start to realize there are dozens of continuity errors like these. You can always do reshoots, but with the number of mistakes there are, you might as well reshoot the majority of your film. You were wearing so many hats during the shoot, and you are confident there was no way you would have been able to catch all of this. If only you or someone else would have devoted their attention to continuity, it would have prevented these errors from happening in the first place.

The Solution

Let's be honest, with everything happening on a film shoot, there is no possible way you can expect yourself to be able to rigorously pay attention to elements of continuity in every scene of your project. Although you may be on a budget or have the desire to work with a skeleton crew, you must consider hiring a script supervisor. Script supervisors take detailed notes on every take from every scene. The notes they take cover everything from the description of the articles of clothing your talent is wearing, the highlighted takes the director liked the best, which line was not read properly by one of your actors, and more. Most importantly, they will have their eyes and ears on everything, leaving you to be able to successfully manage the shoot.

All of the detailed notes the script supervisor procured from the shoot are eventually turned into a daily editor's log. The daily editor's log outlines each individual take and provides detailed information, including notes from the producer and director. For example, it would allow an editor to know the director's favorite performance so the editor will be able to incorporate this particular take in their cut of the film. The script supervisor is also responsible for numbering every shot and making sure the second assistant camera and sound mixer are consistently aware of what shot number they are filming on. This ensures no confusion in post-production organization. They inform talent on any changes in the script or misspoken dialogue to ensure everyone is on the same page. Script supervisors commonly feed lines to actors who are struggling to remember them along with performing line readings in cases where other actors aren't present—for instance, one side of a phone conversation. Lastly, they keep notes of the running time of every shot, keep track of which way actors are looking when they address each other, and create daily logs summarizing which pieces of the film shoot have been successful and which pieces will need to be reshot.

With so many responsibilities of a script supervisor, you without a doubt want to employ someone who has ample experience. Even if your project is on the smaller scale, like a commercial or short film, you must obtain the assistance from a script supervisor with a track record of experience. Conducting the same research methods found in the prospecting stage, be sure to closely analyze this person's work experience, along with carrying out at least two reference checks. It can result in the difference between a successful film and a film with a million mistakes.

Conflict #4

The Obsessive Director With All the Time in the World

The Conflict

You have charted the timeline of your shoot with your first assistant director during pre-production and you are ready to start shooting your project. Everyone is excited, including your director, who has been ready for this day for quite some time. Your director has even done pre-planning of their storyboard and shot list with your director of photography. Everything is going as planned in the beginning, but you start to notice that your director is attempting to make sure everything is perfect before moving on to the next shot or scene. A few hours go by and you check with your assistant director, suddenly realizing you are way behind schedule and you still have two other scenes you need to film before day's end. Your director has been obsessing over every single shot and line of dialogue delivered by your actors, ultimately causing everyone on set to be exhausted and impatient. You and your assistant director are eager to quickly move on with the next item on the schedule, but your director won't get the message. You had the schedule planned to a T, yet you have found yourself in a deep hole of lost time and playing in a game of constant catch-up.

The Solution

The initial solution to this problem is prescribing a simple dose of communication with your director. Sitting your director down as soon as possible and pointing out the excessive amount of time spent on each shot and highlighting how it is negatively impacting the project's planned timeline should be your first mode of action. Pay attention to the tone of voice you are using to communicate this message. You want to make certain you don't come off as combative; instead, you are seeking to set a tone of collaboration. Ask questions and be sure to listen to your director's pain points instead of jumping to suggestions. The two of you are working toward the same goal of producing the project on time and on budget. Sometimes people need a wakeup call due to a lack of awareness of an outsider's perspective.

Another solution you can implement is to hire an experienced assistant director who knows how to effectively command your project's cast and crew and achieve objectives on time and on budget. Novice assistant directors are usually the ones running around the film set and screaming about the lack of time. They are in a constant panic and only contribute more stress than needed. On the other hand, an effective and experienced assistant director is able to calmly instruct the set in an empowering and conducive way. They are constantly planning ahead and accounting for contingencies, all while communicating schedule plans with everyone on a frequent basis. More important, they aren't intimidated by the project's director, and they fully understand their responsibilities revolve around making sure everything moves in accordance with the schedule.

Your crew should also be thinking several steps ahead of what is happening on set. For example, while your director of photography and gaffer are setting up the lights for the next scene, instead of everyone waiting around for them to complete this task, they can get started on what they need to accomplish. The makeup artist and wardrobe person can make the necessary changes with the talent, the director can review their storyboard and shot list, and the first assistant camera can make changes to the camera's lens. This is why it's crucial to perform pre-production tasks like creating a storyboard, shooting schedule, shot list, and lighting plans. By preparing these materials beforehand, you are ensuring time spent on set is productive and meaningful. There is no reason why anyone on set should be standing around with nothing to do. Remember, even if plans do change, which most likely they will, it's better to have some form of strategy in place than having no strategy at all.

Conflict #5

The Inexperienced Gaffer Who Set the Film Set on Fire

The Conflict

You are at the final stretch of your film shoot and can't be more excited to be finished. Working twelve or more hours a day for the past three weeks have been, tough but nothing is more rewarding than making movies with the people you love. Your crew is setting up for the final few shots, and everything appears to be going well until you hear some commotion coming from the area where your gaffer is setting up lights. You quickly run over to discover your gaffer struggling with a Hydrargyrum Medium-Arc Iodide (HMI) light, which emits light in the range of 5,800 Kelvin and uses mercury gas. You know this particular lamp would be very dangerous if dropped, especially while turned on. All your fears come to life before your eyes as the light smashes to the floor. A fire quickly breaks out and spreads to the rest of the equipment surrounding the light, while the gaffer immediately flees to safety. You knew the activity of film-making had its fair share of fires to be put out. However, you didn't expect to be putting out actual fires. Unfortunately, neither you, nor the gaffer, nor anyone else on your cast and crew planned for something like this to happen, which is why you have nothing immediately available to attempt to put the fire out. All you can do is call 9-1-1 and hope the fire department gets to your location before extensive damage is done.

The Solution

Safety should always be on your mind during every stage of the filmmaking process, especially while on a film set filled with highly flammable and dangerous equipment. Everyone's safety is more important than your project, and you must execute the appropriate measures to ensure their well-being. This means that during your pre-production preparation you are actively educating yourself and others around you on health and safety measures. This consists of everything, from understanding how to properly use the camera and lighting equipment; to consulting with stunt coordinators, nurses, and security personnel if needed; to acquiring production insurance that covers you from public injury and property damage caused as a result of filming activity.

Even though you plan to hire crew members who are considered experts in what they do, you should still take the initiative to educate yourself on the potential risks involved with certain types of equipment and procedures. The electrical department consists of your gaffer, who is responsible for regulating all electrical use on set. This includes the lights illuminating your set, the craft service's microwave, talent trailers, and more. Usually, on an ultra-low-budget independent film the number of personnel available to you is limited. However, in the case of anything related to electricity, you should at least have a professional gaffer on set. The gaffer is the head of the electrical department and works directly under the director of photography, assisting in developing and building the film's lighting plan on a shoot. Your gaffer is working with an abundant amount of potentially hazardous equipment like lights, hardware tools, and tech gadgets. This is why it's crucial to employ someone who not only has the appropriate equipment but knows how to correctly and safely use it.

When it comes to on-set safety, you should also perform a detailed inspection during your tech scout of the location during pre-production. Your assistant director should join and perform what is called a tech recce, which consists of organizing health and safety measures required before principal photography takes place. During your pre-production paperwork, you should also perform a detailed risk assessment, which is a legal document highlighting the possible health and safety risks and hazards that may occur on set. When documenting how you aim to make the film set safe, also be sure to share it with every single member of your crew before filming commences. You should also administer accident and incident report forms and highlight safety instructions in your daily call sheets. Always provide the nearest hospital and medical emergency center contact information on your call sheets so everyone is aware of where to go if an incident occurs. If your script consists of complex stunts and special effects like fire or smoke, make sure you have the presence of personnel like safety supervisors, stunt coordinators, and medical professionals.

Case Study—A Final Word on Relationship Success

There are various other conflicts that can possibly occur during the filmmaking process. From creative differences with a screenwriter you have hired for a rewrite to a horrific movie poster created by the marketing department of your film's distributor, problems can form any time between development and the exhibition of your final product. It's not a question of *if* conflicts will occur but more so how and what you will do to solve conflicts when they arise. The final stage in the sales process, relationship success, is all about how you deal with the individuals around you, while also looking after each other's best interests. It's a stage centering on your ability to influence those around you in a positive way.

When dealing with conflicts with your crew members, remember to accept and analyze the conflict. Don't attempt to discredit it and shove it under the rug. Ask yourself why this is happening in the first place. By no means are you expected to be perfect in every situation, especially if it's a situation you have never encountered before. However, you can choose to learn from the conflicts you are subject to and chalk these occurrences up to experience. Educate yourself as much as you possibly can to mitigate any sort of risk leading to conflict. You also want to surround yourself with knowledgeable and experienced individuals who can get the job done instead of amateurs who will give you more headaches than you can count. Instead of lazily going with the flow and hoping things turn out okay, you need to take the initiative to strategize the possibilities of every single element of your project. Preparation is the key to success and without it, you will find yourself extinguishing fires left and right.

Relationship success is the culmination of being a good human being. In the sales process of identifying an individual's pain points and goals, demonstrating the value you can bring to the table, and committing yourself to a successful relationship, you have finally reached the most important component. Relationship success is all about empowering those around you and assisting them in reaching their goals and dreams. The best part is that through the act of helping others reach their full potential, you are indirectly helping yourself realize your goals and objectives. Instead of selfishly looking out for yourself, true sales results in healthy and prosperous partnerships that positively impact both parties. As a filmmaker, whether you are dealing with a screenwriter, cinematographer, lawyer, or financier, the aim is to establish a long-standing fruitful partnership, elevating both of you to levels you have never seen before.

THE FINAL WORD

Sales has become a negative word in today's culture. From the greedy Gorden Gekko archetype who is purely motivated by money and power, to the snake oil salesman who will dish out lie after lie until you have signed on the dotted line, there are a variety of stereotypes that feed into the negative perception of salespeople. However, for every misrepresentation of a salesperson found in our culture (often constructed by the media), there are also honest ones who genuinely devote their time and energy to solving the problems and achieving the goals of their clients. These righteous salespeople are found across the world, in major cities, little towns, and even in our mirrors.

———

The truth is, we all are in sales. Whether it is with your family, friends, acquaintances, or co-workers, you are performing sales techniques with or without conscious awareness. Every day we are selling the people around us through actions like checking out the first episode of a fourteen-season television show, purchasing an expensive engagement ring to demonstrate your love, or preparing for a job interview with a Fortune 500 company. You even sell yourself on certain beliefs, values, and opinions that you have established throughout the years. Sales is as much a part of your daily habits as eating, sleeping, and breathing.

As an independent filmmaker, you are selling others on yourself and the stories you produce and share with the world. From Quentin Tarantino's ability to network with Lawrence Bender and others from his circle of influence, to Steven Spielberg's propensity to establish rapport and trust with individuals like Sid Sheinberg and Chuck Silvers, sales is a part of the filmmaking process as much as pressing the RECORD button on a camera or writing the first few lines of dialogue in a screenplay.

The Five Stages of the Sales Process

There are five distinct phases in the sales process one must follow to ensure they are effectively listening to their prospect's problems and goals in order to provide a project or service that will correctly benefit them. These five stages also happen to also exist in every area of the filmmaking process.

Stage 1—Prospecting: Consists of the process of searching for the best person who would find value in your project or service. Whether it's through phone, email, or in person, prospecting is the act of putting yourself out there. In independent filmmaking, this can include a screenwriter in search for a producer, a producer in search of the right distributor, or a sound editor in search of their next gig. The main goals of prospecting are:

- Connecting with the ideal person and/or company

- Decreasing the amount of wasted time with people who don't benefit from the value of your project or service

- Using your research to communicate your knowledge of your prospect's background and experience

Stage 2—Discovery: Strategically focused on building rapport and identifying your prospect's pain points and goals. From understanding a cinematographer's or a director's vision for a commercial, to a producer acknowledging a screenwriter's personal goals for their award-winning screenplay, to a filmmaker recognizing a potential location owner's pain points, the main objectives of discovery are:

- Building rapport and establishing a relationship with your prospect

- Unearthing your prospect's pain points and personal goals

- Vetting your prospect to ensure they are a good fit for your project or service

Stage 3—Demonstrating Value: The act of displaying how your project or service will directly benefit your prospect based on what you have learned in the previous stage. As a filmmaker you will find yourself doing this when presenting a pitch deck to a financier, demonstrating your experience as an editor, or showcasing your feature film to a distributor. When demonstrating value you are:

- Putting the needs and goals of your prospect first

- Using methods to articulate the value of your product or service

- Establishing yourself as a source of expertise on your industry, project, or service

Stage 4—Closing the Deal: Centered on asking for the prospect's commitment, answering all of their concerns, and getting an agreement finalized in writing. This can be demonstrated in addressing an actress's list of objections before giving her the part, asking a prospective client for agreement in the video services you have offered them, or finalizing legal documents before a financier hands over a check. Closing the deal covers:

- Handling any of your prospect's objections and eliminating any sort of fears

- Asking for their business and invoking a sense of urgency

- Establishing your agreement in writing with a legally binding contract

Stage 5—Relationship Success: Revolves around keeping your clients and business partners happy, along with delivering the value you have demonstrated throughout the previous stages of the sales process. From a freelance filmmaker actively checking in with their client, to a producer resolving conflicts with their cast and crew, to a director employing a positive attitude in response to adversity, relationship success is a two-way process that positively impacts all parties involved. Relationship success ensures you are:

- Keeping your client actively in the loop on relevant developments and updates

- Resolving conflicts that may arise at any point during the relationship

- Using a positive attitude to exceed client expectations and garner upsell opportunities

Embracing Sales in Independent Filmmaking

Where do you go from here? It's a simple answer that will result in endless opportunities. Whether you are a freelance director of photography looking for your next gig, an indie producer about to shoot your next feature film, or a novice screenwriter launching your writing career, it's imperative that you confidently accept that you are a salesperson as well.

Going forward, be sure to apply the five stages of the sales process throughout your filmmaking journey. Every individual you meet along the way should be looked at as a prospect, with the hopes of turning them into a thriving client. Take the time to do your research, identify what they believe is important, and exhibit the many ways you can help them. Continually build upon your relationships and actively identify ways you can provide value. Think about how your project or service compares with other opportunities, and most importantly, how your project or service will positively impact them.

By implementing the sales strategies outlined in this book you will be able to acquire more opportunities, open more doors, and continue to follow your passions and dreams on a grander scale. Developing and internalizing a sales mindset will also assist you in advancing your craft or business and create a better life for yourself and the people around you.

So next time you hear the words "lights … camera" on a film shoot, remember to take *action* and go out there and *sell*!

SPECIAL THANKS

To the great companies and managers I have worked for, thank you for all of the opportunities.

To the amazing clients I have had the pleasure to work with, thank you for all that I have learned from you and the success we shared and continue to share.

To my Mom and Dad, thank you for your support. I'm eternally grateful for your everlasting encouragement.

To Jessica, for her immortal love and support of my filmmaking and business ambitions.

To the independent filmmakers who have crossed my path, thank you for making this world a more exciting and interesting place to live.

ABOUT THE AUTHOR

Alec Trachtenberg is an independent film producer, author, sales consultant, and the founder and CEO of Coast ART Productions. Born and raised in New York, Alec has always had a passion for sales, entrepreneurship, and filmmaking.

With over a decade of experience working in sales at some of the most cutting-edge companies, Alec has built prosperous relationships with his clients, such as Airbnb, Sony Pictures, Netflix, and Amazon. He has directly generated millions of dollars in revenue for a variety of companies in the technology, entertainment, and digital marketing industries. In addition, Alec consults freelancers, small business owners, and entrepreneurs from all walks of life and shows them how to multiply their profits.

Through his production company, Coast ART Productions, Alec has produced a variety of short films and the international feature horror film *The Cabin* (2018). He currently resides in Los Angeles, California. Learn more about Alec at alectrachtenberg.com

Made in the USA
Las Vegas, NV
04 August 2021